FILM REVIEW

by

F·MAURICE SPEED

MACDONALD & CO (*Publishers*) LTD, 19, LUDGATE HILL, E.C.4

CONTENTS

Koda by Wilfrid Newton

Most important as well as the most expensive British movie of the year has been LAURENCE OLIVIER'S second attempt to put Shakespeare on the screen, his superbly lavish, intelligent, interesting and controversial HAMLET. Here OLIVIER (who directed and produced the picture) is seen in the title role, as the mentally tortured Prince of Denmark.

INTRODUCTION

AT this point in the production of FILM REVIEW, when each year I sit down at my typewriter to write these words of Introduction, I get the feeling that I'm about to talk (or write, if you prefer it) to so many old friends. The feeling is inescapable in that during the five years that I have been compiling this annual I have received many thousands of letters, and each year I note that a considerable proportion of these letters bear the same signatures.

These old friends, then, will hardly want to read the next couple of paragraphs, which are intended primarily for any newcomers who may be just about to read through a FILM REVIEW for the first time. For them—and for old readers with short memories of course—let me once again outline the purpose of this volume.

First and foremost the aim is to present a comprehensive record of the year in the cinema ; to produce, in as entertaining a manner as possible, a complete, convenient and fully illustrated list of the year's films—who made them, who appeared in them, who directed and produced them, and the date they were first released ; also to record something of the year's more important cinematic events. A subsidiary, but also quite important, purpose is to look into the future and see what it has to offer to us moviegoers in 1949.

Again, as with every prior edition of FILM REVIEW, you will here and there discover minor modifications in format or content. You may find a small feature dropped altogether, or another introduced ; even your favourite section may be wearing a New Look. But you'll find that all these changes are relatively quite unimportant. The main character of the volume remains the same, its primary object is still to combine in one book enough of two worlds to make it of general interest and attraction today and a book of steady reference use tomorrow, and in the years to come.

Lastly the usual word of thanks to the many letter-writers. Though it has again been something of a major headache for my secretary and myself, we have managed to answer personally each writer during the year. I greatly appreciate the many ideas and suggestions—all helpful, all interesting—which have again been sent to me. I hope you won't be too disappointed if your suggestion hasn't been incorporated in this volume. You see, it is impossible to act on any but a few of the many ideas I receive each year. But I am grateful for them all the same, as even if I haven't used your ideas this time I might be able to introduce them at some future date.

Which brings me to a footnote. Many readers write asking for colour plates of their favourite film stars and sometimes comment (occasionally rather rudely !) on my choice in this matter. Well, in excuse, let me say that nearly all of you appear to have different ideas on the subject and, anyway, I am confined to the material available. If you can't find in this year's FILM REVIEW a portrait of the star *you* think I ought to have included, it probably just means that a colour still, or Kodachrome, of that particular star wasn't available. Yes, it is mostly as simple as that. So until next year best wishes and, again, many, many thanks.

IN many ways 1948 has been a momentous year in the history of the cinema. And in the years to come, when we look back at it, I feel it may well prove of even greater import than it seems to us right now—certainly the full impact of some of the events of the past twelve months will not be fully felt for some time.

The year started depressingly enough, heaven knows. The 75 per cent tax on all imported films, imposed by the Board of Trade in 1947, had been quickly followed by the American counter-move of stopping all her Hollywood film productions from entering this country just so long as it remained in force.

So as 1948 dawned we faced a somewhat dreary cinematic future. It appeared inevitable that after the few remaining, pre-tax, American movies had been shown, all we should have to see in our cinemas would be a succession of revivals of yesteryear's pictures, interspersed, of course, with our own new productions.

It was a controversial tax. Some people over here saw it as a danger to the British cinema and, in the long run, even a danger to the British film. But it was also, look at it from whichever angle you might, a really great opportunity for the British film producers. If the tax remained, and if the Hollywood attitude did not soften, then soon our cinemas would be looking around greedily for every new British film they could get. In those circumstances one might have well expected a sudden, almost violent upsurge in British production figures. Actually the reverse was the case. British production lagged sadly and at once, (although the Rank group of companies remained as busy as ever with their programme of 40 films). Money became tighter almost overnight and independent producers found it almost impossible to get the financial backing they needed. A strange feeling of apathy crept through the British film industry, and remained firmly embedded until the eventual repeal of the tax.

During the interim, move was followed by

One of the sadder events of the year was the untimely death of the grand old Scots character-actor Will Fyffe. The fact that all his scenes in the Alexander Korda production of Bonnie Prince Charlie *had to be re-shot was one of the main factors for the delay of the film. Here is one of the last photographs to be taken of Fyffe, as he chats to producer Alexander Korda between scenes on location.*

Director Alfred Hitchcock consults his continuity girl while stars Ann Todd and Ethel Barrymore prepare for the next shot of the David O. Selznick production The Paradine Case.

counter-move, each preceded by a barrage of rumours. Hollywood producers could see the tax only as a savage and direct British thrust at them and they could not seem to understand that we just hadn't got the dollars to pay out the millions of pounds that had previously gone across the Atlantic every year to purchase our celluloid entertainment.

Eventually the tax was settled at highest level. Over from America came Eric Johnston, President of the Motion Picture Association of America, to try and find a permanent compromise solution in co-operation with British Board of Trade president Harold Wilson. The discussions were always realistic. Later, tough Eric Johnston admitted that Wilson was the toughest negotiator he had come up against. But after twelve days of argument and suggestions, on Thursday, March 11th, Harold Wilson announced the repeal of the tax in the House of Commons. The settlement terms, in brief, were : The tax should be withdrawn and the normal import of American films should be resumed as soon as possible. But, and here was the important proviso, not more than seventeen million dollars should be remitted to the U.S.A. from Britain each year, this plus a sum equal to the earnings of the British films in America. The unremitted balance of dollars was to remain in this country to be used by the Americans in a number of different ways. So peace was declared.

It had come just in time. In the cinemas the moviegoers were showing that they were getting just a little tired of seeing the endless procession of revivals. Takings were dropping. In the West End of London business was worse than bad. On occasions I myself saw less than a dozen people in the circle of one of London's most famous cinemas.

Almost at once, after the terms had been agreed, the Trade papers announced that the American companies had some 265 new feature films ready to rush to Britain. But there was no rush. On the contrary, it soon became obvious that both sides were going to start by feeling their way slowly. For one thing, the British cinema circuits' emergency plans, under which they had booked considerable numbers of revivals, extended well into the autumn and they were somewhat naturally loath suddenly to switch their schedules.

Indeed, if there was to be a flood of American movies, it started with a most deceptive trickle. Distinction of showing the first post-tax film went to Metro-Goldwyn-Mayer, who on May 13 screened at their Empire cinema the comedy *The Bride Goes Wild* ; to be followed by Universal-International's *A Double Life* (the film which won Ronald Colman his first " Oscar " for the best male screen performance of the year) at the Leicester Square Theatre a week later.

But no sooner was the tax trouble settled than a new reason for bad feeling cropped up. This was the new British Quota Act. More of this later, however.

Turning for a moment to matters technical, here

again it has been an interesting year and one that historians may in the future quite possibly claim to have been an important one for at least three developments. First of these was the tremendous advance made in the production of a non-inflammable film for commercial showing. Long produced for non-commercial, amateur uses, non-inflammable stock had never been yet successfully used on 35mm. film. The advantages of such an innovation must be obvious even to a layman. Anyway, in May, Gevaert revealed that their factory in Antwerp was then organized to produce maximum requirements of acitate butyrate safety base and that all their ciné films could then be produced on this material. At about the same time Kodak announced that their experiments in the same direction had reached the commercial stage.

Second possible revolution in the film was the announcement in Paris of the discovery of a new colour process. This was developed by Armonde and Luciene Roux. If as good as it was claimed (and personally I am taking the claims with the greatest possible reserve) it may well suddenly bring forward by a number of years the inevitable moment when all films will be made in colour. For the great point about the process developed by the Roux brothers is that to all intents and purposes it overcomes the present disadvantage of the colour film, by costing no more to produce than its black and white brother. Apparently all it involves is a special lens on the camera and a similar one on the projector ; normal black and white film stock is used and the system consists of focusing different primary colours on different planes in the thickness of the film.

Third technical achievement was the commencement of several productions under the " Independent Frame " process. During the past year or two great secrecy has surrounded the small experimental group which under the Rank banner was planning to make films by this process. But, actually, there was no need for any of this secrecy for the process—if you like to call it that—is very simple. The whole point about it is that by super-careful planning and the extended use of common sense, the cost of any given film can be very considerably reduced. One important factor in the scheme is the reduction of set building and the development of back projection to a greater degree of perfection than ever seen before. It is impossible at this time and place to go into the subject more thoroughly, as to describe all the various implications of the process would take several thousand words and, in any case, these words would be of little interest to any except technicians and those on the production and financial side of the films. But it looks like an important step forward in reducing costs, all the more essential when budgets have grown so terrifyingly large.

One of the more ambitious (and certainly one of the greatest) of the 1948 Rank productions has been the film of the famous Charles Dickens story Oliver Twist. *Here is Cineguild's director David Lean, with his 21-year-old " discovery " Josephine Stuart, who plays Oliver's mother in the picture.*

Starry line-up at the Soup Kitchen counter! Vivien Leigh, Alexander Korda, David Niven, Anthony Kimmins and Kieron Moore queue for their "help yourself" lunch at the London Film Studios Canteen at Shepperton studios.

Now, as promised earlier, something about the new Quota Act, an act which once again set American producers in an uproar and was the cause of many cross-Atlantic protests and threats. As you probably already know, the original Quota Act makes it necessary for every British cinema to show a certain percentage of British movies each year. This Act expired in October and apart from any other consideration it was necessary to reconsider the percentage figures for British and foreign films necessary to renew it either in the form in which it was then cast or with new percentages. Actually the number of British films each cinema must show within a year was quite considerably increased. In the future 45 per cent of the first feature films and 25 per cent of the supporting pictures must be British. These figures were a little breath-taking. Even at the old percentage (roughly half the new) many cinemas had been—or had claimed to have been—unable to keep within the law and they now stoutly alleged that the new figure was ridiculous. America, startled to discover that it would mean each company would have to reduce its features sent here to under the dozen a year, reacted quite naturally with a howl of protest, threatening to renew the only recently raised ban of their films. Rank, obviously pleased, also made an announcement, to the effect that he was planning to meet the situation by releasing some 60 films during the first twelve-month quota period.

*   *   *   *   *

NOW, before I pass on to talk about some of the more interesting movies of the past year there are one or two events of major, and minor, importance which I feel are worthy of mention in any record of the filmic year.

For instance, two of the sadder news items of the year concerned the deaths of movie pioneers. In Russia, at the age of 49, died famous director Sergei Eisenstein. Eisenstein earned his place in any history of the movies with that classic of the silent screen *Battleship Potemkin*, and, more recently, with his large-scale talkie *Alexander Nevski*.

Then, a few months later (in June) we heard from France that the first Frenchman of the cinema, Louis Lumiere, had died on the Riviera at the ripe old age of 83. It was way back in 1895 that Louis, in collaboration with elder brother Auguste, gave his first demonstration of the "cinématographe" and before the end of that year had opened a makeshift cinema, first in France, in the basement of The Grand Café in Paris. Louis went on experimenting and in 1903 presented the French Academy of Sciences with a practical process for colour films. In fact, the modern film, in its present glory of glossy perfection, owes much to the painstaking and difficult early experimenting of Louis Lumiere and the few like him.

Another interesting development behind the

*See also page 145.

scenes during the year, was the purchase of the controlling interest in R.K.O. Radio by multi-millionaire Howard Hughes. Hughes, a young man of ideas and courage, designer and builder of the famous Constellation Airliners, has always taken an interest in the movies. It was from him that came two of the more sensational pictures of the last 20 years, *Hell's Angels* (which introduced Jean Harlow to the screen) and *The Outlaw* (which first brought Jane Russell—rather literally—into public view).

In America another event of the year was the investigation of Hollywood "Reds" by the so called Un-American Activities Investigation Committee. By it America, in her efforts to stamp out Communism in the film colony, drove out several of her finest producers and directors.

Over here one of the more gloomy occasions of 1948 was the going out of business of British National, so long associated with the Boreham Wood Studios. To British National we owe a number of fine British films through the years (*Love on the Dole* and *One of Our Aircraft is Missing* among them) and some very interesting ones. But, more recently, National seemed to have lost the magic touch and I don't think any of us was greatly surprised when the announcement came that Lady Yule, who had financed the studios' output for so long, had decided to cease production.

Another British event worthy of special mention is the formation of the British Film Academy. This is too important to be dismissed here in a few lines and elsewhere in this volume you will find a special feature devoted to the Academy, its formation, objects and first activities.

During the year one very bad phase in picture making has been continued ; the habit of making films too long. So often a movie which otherwise might have been entertaining enough became a sheer bore because of the manner in which it was painfully drawn out. In America a move has already started for shorter films and I think it is a move which could spread over here. For the unanswerable fact remains that it is far more than twice as difficult to make a 2 hour film as entertaining as one that lasts 60 minutes.

To conclude this section I can't resist mentioning a cinema innovation which has recently taken place in Japan. Apparently one of the cinema managers over there was struck by the number of young couples who went to his cinema to hold hands as well as see the film—or in some cases instead of seeing it ! Apparently this manager had an eye to business, for he decided to cash in on young romance. He has now installed in his cinema a series of twin, so called "romance" seats, for which he charges 80 yen instead of the usual 20 yen it costs to buy a single seat. And now he's doing great business. I pass the idea on to any British cinema manager who might care or would dare to copy it.

* * * * *

Since I wrote the foregoing, another important cinematic milestone has been announced, confirming

This "production shot" from Columbia's It Had To Be You, *starring Cornel Wilde and Ginger Rogers, shows something of the difficulties under which film players labour when they are called upon to "emote"—to use a popular Americanism—for a scene. Gent apparently taking it easy in the white suit is producer-director Don Hartman.*

Another idea of the kind of thing a film player is up against when acting those difficult intimate scenes for the camera. In focus is Sally Gray, while looking at her through the eyepiece is camera and lighting expert Erwin Hillier. At his shoulder is director Brian Desmond Hurst. The film is the Two Cities production Mark of Cain.

the historical importance of 1948. This has been the announcement of a Government plan to set up a Film Finance Corporation, with £5,000,000 to lend to independent producers.

In doing this the Board of Trade's Harold Wilson said that it had become an urgent need to make such a move in view of the City's reluctance to loan money for such purposes and the national necessity that British Film production must continue. If the scheme were a success, and the loans came back quickly enough, it might later be possible to increase the sum available for borrowing.

It is too late for me to comment upon this new and somewhat controversial move. But the implications are obvious. For the first time British films will be made on finance advanced as a loan by the Government, thus assuring that enough British pictures be made to give exhibitors no chance to put forward the plea that not enough home-made movies are available to allow them to keep to their quota commitments.

* * *

IN any discussion of the 1948 films it is as well, I think, to divide them into two distinct sections. In the first half of the year the tax, and the resulting Hollywood ban, was in force, so apart from a few pre-tax movies stored in their London vaults by the more fortunate of the American companies, most of the new movies for general release originated in our own studios. Then, in June the tax was

repealed and the ban was lifted; the flow of American movies to this country started once again.

Of the British pictures in the first group few were outstanding, though a number of them offered generally excellent entertainment. One of the best of these early releases (strictly speaking its actual release date came at the very tail end of 1947) was *It Always Rains on Sunday*. This careful, observant study of East End life bore the touch of genius. Its characters were believable, its action normal and its background authentic. I should rate it high in any list of British movies.

A quite unusual and rather interesting production of this first period was *Corridor of Mirrors*, a film with a history. Star Edana Romney—who helped produce and also assisted in the writing of the script—had decided to make the film several years ago but was always prevented from doing so by various unfortunate hold-ups. For instance, for a long time it was a question of getting the financial backing and even when this was obtained studio space proved unavailable. Disgusted, but always still grimly determined, Miss Romney moved the whole set-up to Paris and made the movie there. It proved a very strange but quite an unusually lovely one I thought. It bore the stamp of artistic integrity, for one gathered the impression that everyone concerned with the movie had tried desperately hard to keep the production up to a high artistic level. And they succeeded well enough to make *Corridor of Mirrors* one of the better British films of the year.

[continued on page 15

Flashback! DANNY KAYE, author of the article on the following page, as he appeared with VIRGINIA MAYO in KID FROM BROOKLYN. Though we saw no new DANNY KAYE films in 1948 his *R.K.O. Radio* pictures UP IN ARMS and WONDER MAN proved two of the most successful revivals of the year.

Recipe for Laughter

BY

DANNY KAYE

It is typical of DANNY KAYE that when I asked him to write a " Recipe for Laughter " for me he should turn in the article you are about to read below. For instead of writing about himself, the films he has made or is yet to make, the methods by which he raises the storms of laughter which are the inevitable tribute to his always perfectly clean, clever humour, Danny Kaye chose to take the opportunity of once again thanking the British public for the reception it gave him when he appeared personally for a season at the Palladium and elsewhere in this country last February. It is to the audience that Danny gives the credit, which is typical of his nature, even if quite unfair to his own very considerable talent. Never has an American artist had a greater reception and success in this country and never has an artist been more deeply and truly grateful for that reception. Danny Kaye is a fine artist, a fine comedian and a fine gentleman ; he is 35, born New York (Brooklyn). His first appearance on the screen was in Samuel Goldwyn's " Up in Arms."

WRITING is one of the things I don't do well. When asked to write an article titled " Recipe for Laughter," my first inclination was to run and hide behind the nearest beer barrel. On second thought I realized this article offered me the opportunity to talk on the record about the greatest recipe for laughter I have ever encountered in all of the twenty-two years I have been entertaining throughout the world, namely, the wonderfully warm people who attended my performances at the Palladium Theatre.

Most of the theatre-going public never realize the greatest contribution to an artist's performance never comes from himself, but rather from his audience.

I have seen a great many talented performers go out on the stage time after time, prepared to give of their all, only to be stymied by a particularly cold audience that is unappreciative ; and their lack of feeling is immediately transmitted to the performer, in return his creativeness is considerably dampened, with the result that both the performer and the audience create an impenetrable barrier between them. I will admit that the good performer will fight to break down this barrier and many times he succeeds in doing this to the mutual satisfaction of both the audience and the performer.

However, this was never my experience in London. From the very first performance on February 2, right through to my closing performance, I encountered only tremendous appreciation both personal and show-wise. The impact of this warmth and appreciation was doubly so to me. Just as a great many people think the true American is best represented by a loud, aggressive, over-dressed individual, so do a great many Americans think that Englishmen are represented by the motion picture type of Briton, namely, the cold, reserved and aloof person. I must confess that I also was a little guilty of this. Hence, when I came to England the early part of this year and was given the chance to feel the people as such, I was not only wonderfully surprised but emotionally touched.

Vaudeville or variety, as it is called in your country, is a dead institution here in the States. I am one of many who long to see it return, but I must admit that this seems completely impossible. It might return in a minor form through television, which is making such tremendous strides here in America. However, variety's greatest blessing was that it taught a performer how to become a part of the audience and the audience a part of the performer.

I remember as a child, being taken to the local variety house every week and how this procedure was part of our life at home. The tremendous excitement that used to exist when we knew that in a week or two a Sophie Tucker, a Bill Robinson, or an Eddie Cantor was to appear at " our " theatre. We felt that for this particular week these great stars belonged to us and when my father and mother and brothers would go to the theatre, we went with a feeling of ownership. That was the great feeling I have reference to. When we entered the theatre, we went to see " our " star, and as a result, every other act on the bill gained by that feeling.

Today that is a thing of the past. We don't have vaudeville, and the personal appearances, aside from those regularly made by the American orchestras, are confined to a few key cities with big stars appearing occasionally. Naturally this has led to an appreciation of talent only through the more mechanical means, namely, the screen, radio and phonograph records. This all brings me back to that wonderful feeling I experienced as I sat in the Palladium and watched Sid Field perform, looked around at the audience, the lights, the stage and the orchestra in the pit, and I felt from the audience at the Palladium that Sid Field was also mine. It was the audience that gave me that feeling, and it was a warmth that I carried on stage with me when I opened at the Palladium on February 2. I'll admit I was nervous, as who wouldn't be the first night, but the audience soon made that nervousness disappear and their reaction and acceptance of me was " the greatest recipe for laughter " I have ever experienced.

AROUND WITH DANNY KAYE . . .

In the first picture you see Danny playing host to the Goldwyn Girls on their return from a trip to Europe . . . don't take any notice of that yawn, it's a phoney! In the second picture Danny is obviously having trouble with his pet dog; while in the third, visiting comic Red Skelton has a chat with Danny, leading lady Virginia Mayo and director Norman Z. McLeod on the set of R.K.O. Radio's Technicolored musical The Secret Life of Walter Mitty, the next Kaye picture.

gave an extremely polished and sympathetic performance in the long, central role. Peter Ustinov, a brilliant young man whose brilliance, unfortunately, has not yet advanced beyond the promising stage gave us *Vice Versa*. Here again was promise unfulfilled, mainly because Ustinov kept rigidly to a parochial form of humour which left most people out of the charmed circle tremendously unamused.

One of the most intelligent movies of this period came from the Korda Studio. This was an Anthony Kimmins production—he also directed—of *Mine Own Executioner*. This was based on one of those now all-too-familiar, psychological problems which the movies have revelled in again and again during the past year or so. But in this case the problem was real and the approach intellectual. These factors, allied to some fine acting by Burgess Meredith as a lay psychiatrist, and Kieron Moore as a difficult patient, made this one of the best films that Britain had produced for quite a while.

Britain had more American film star visitors during 1948 than during any other year since before the war. Many of them came to make films here—Ray Milland, Spencer Tracy, Claude Rains and Fredric March among them. March came to make Christopher Columbus *for Sydney Box and he is seen here at the first meeting. While he discusses script with Box, wife Florence Eldridge looks on—she also has a part in the picture.*

Also of this period were the two critically attacked pictures *No Orchids for Miss Blandish* and *Idol of Paris*. In the former case at least the critics waxed more violent than they had done for some considerable time—as a result the queues outside the cinemas made records!

The Year in the Cinema, *continued from page* 11]

Otherwise there was nothing really outstanding. Cineguild wasted superlative production qualities and extremely good Technicolor on an old fashioned melodrama called *Blanche Fury*. Ealing Studios offered *Against the Wind*, a good but somewhat strangely dated film about the Belgian Underground movement during the war. Alexander Korda came across with his Technicolored adaptation of Wilde's *An Ideal Husband* and a magnificently lavish, and dreary, screen version of *Anna Karenina*. The Boulting Brothers made *Brighton Rock* which, as with Cineguild's *Blanche Fury*, seemed to me to be a rather shocking waste of money, time and talent on what was basically a rather unsuitable story.

Very good, if not quite outstanding, was Associated British's *My Brother Jonathan*, the rather tender story of a young doctor who sets out with high ideals and ambitions of a Harley Street practice but whose humanity in the end sidetracks him into the life of a general practitioner in a highly industrialised, gloomy Northern Town. This picture introduced to the screen one of the most promising young male stars we have had for a long time, for in it newcomer Michael Denison

At Shepherds Bush and Islington Sydney Box continued to turn out films at an astonishing rate—and also on a surprisingly high level. Soon he had passed—and raised—his own target of twelve films a year. Some of these films, let's face it, were of a very medium calibre. But some of them were very good. For instance, *Miranda*, the story of a " man-eating " mermaid, proved funnier in the film than it was in the original play. *Easy Money*, a story of the football pools was another excellent production and even *Good Time Girl*, coming at an awkward moment—at the time when *No Orchids* had caused a critical uproar about bad taste on the screen—overcame any pre-conceived antipathy to its subject and was generally acclaimed as an excellent job of work. In fact, large, genial, always astute and intelligent Sydney was doing, better than one could imagine anyone else could, the job of supplying Mr. Rank's twin circuits with a steady succession of money-making pictures.

The first half of the year, though it saw few American films released, did offer some good ones. For instance, it was in this period that we saw the new Chaplin, *Monsieur Verdoux*, which met with fairly mixed reception from the critics but was undoubtedly one of the more intelligent, thoughtful pictures to come out of Hollywood during the year. Though now more serious in intent, anxious to show the world where it is going wrong, Chaplin remains the greatest clown of them all, and even if he wanted to—which I doubt—could not help some of the sequences in the movie being exquisitely funny.

Also released early in the year was the delightful new Disney *Fun and Fancy Free* (in which the maestro took a step backward towards his *Bambi* style) and *The Best Years of Our Lives*, that great Goldwyn film about the men who came back from the war. Quite unassailable in its class, this. We should be grateful, too, for the Orson Welles picture *Lady from Shanghai* which, in spite of its defects, was unusual and intelligent enough to make it well worth noting.

Crossfire touched delicately—some said too hesitatingly—upon the topical problem of anti-Semitism in America. It did this by way of making it the reason for a murder unravelled by thoughtful detective Robert Young. Unsatisfactory in many ways, *Crossfire* deserves credit for coming off the fence and taking sides on a thorny subject.

The Hope-Crosby-Lamour team appeared during this period in another " Road " film, *Road to Rio*.

Warner's *Unfaithful* had Ann Sheridan as a left-at-home war wife who in a weak moment commits a single, regretted, indiscretion and has to considerably suffer from it. It is a topical—and even quite common—problem after any war and the Warner film dealt with it both conscientiously and well.

Last of the American films of this period I want to mention is a more modest production which was made by R.K.O. Radio, called *Indian Summer*. I enjoyed it immensely, possibly because it starred two of my favourite screen players in Alexander Knox and Ann Sothern. But, in any case, it was a charming story and the treatment had a fresh, open-air atmosphere about it which was quite unusual.

Then, as I have previously said, the tax was repealed and the ban lifted and across the Atlantic the flow of American films started once more. Amongst the first batch there were a number of gems to prove that any talk about Hollywood " slipping " was considerably premature—to say the least. The first film, brought here by M-G-M. to their Empire cinema, was *The Bride Goes Wild*, a not unamusing little comedy with Van Johnson and June Allyson. In fact, it had quite a number of good laughs and that's something British films were singularly in short supply at that time. Then

[continued on page 143

One of the more important 1948 movies is The Lost Illusion *directed by Carol Reed (of* Way Ahead *and* Odd Man Out *fame) for Sir Alexander Korda. Here is star Ralph Richardson carefully toeing the white line which keeps him in focus—during location filming in Belgrave Square. Director Reed is to be seen squatting on the camera trolley.*

Unfortunate SUSAN PETERS, doomed by a hunting accident to act her future roles in a wheel chair, and ALEXANDER KNOX in *Columbia's* SIGN OF THE RAM.

MUSIC IN BRITISH FILMS

by

MUIR MATHIESON

Music Director of the J. Arthur Rank Organisation—was born in Stirling, Scotland in 1911. He first began to conduct with the Stirling Boys Orchestra when he was 13 years old and did his first B.B.C. Broadcast from the Glasgow Station of the B.B.C. Then he won two scholarships and went to the Royal College of Music.

On leaving the college he began work as Assistant Music Director to Alexander Korda at the age of 20, subsequently becoming Music Director for London Films. His first picture was the *Life of Don Juan* made in 1934. There followed a whole series of famous films for which Mathieson directed the music, among them *The Ghost Goes West, Thief of Bagdad, Things to Come, Sanders of the River*, etc.

Throughout the war years he directed the music for a large number of pictures and was in charge of this branch of film-making for R.A.F., Army and Crown Film Units. Since then he has directed music for many films : *The Rake's Progress, Seventh Veil, Brief Encounter, Men of Two Worlds, Odd Man Out, Hamlet* and *Oliver Twist* to mention but a few. In all he has been responsible for the music in well over 300 British films.

In addition to films Muir Mathieson has conducted concerts of the leading British orchestras in many parts of the country. Muir Mathieson was married in 1936 to Hermione Darnborough, a ballet dancer with Sadler's Wells ; they have three children, aged 3, 5 and 9.

Muir Mathieson, Music Director of the J. Arthur Rank Organisation.

MUSIC and the cinema have always been inseparable from the very beginning. Although music does not need the films, it seems that the films have always needed music. For example, it is recorded that the very first public film show presented in 1895 in Paris by the Lumiere Brothers was accompanied by improvisations on the piano, while even as early as 1908 we find Saint-Saens writing a special score for the Paris performance of " The Assassination of the Duke of Guise," a production of the " Film d'Art" company. 1911 saw the first specially composed music for a film in America (by Walter Cleveland Simon) and two years later Joseph Carl Breil prepared his 165 minutes of music for " Birth of a Nation," the famous silent epic made by D. W. Griffiths. In fact, there never was such a thing as a " silent " cinema, for really " silent films " have little or no entertainment value at all without some accompanying sound—and up to 1928, that sound was music.

The coming of talkies disposed of the " incidental " music at first, but after a time it returned with renewed vigour once again to give added dramatic impact, to sweeten, to liven up, to underline, to complement action and movement, to enhance the art of film-making. This time, however, there was a difference, for the cinema had reached a new state in its development when serious-minded contemporary composers and progressive film producers got together to ensure that only the very best music should go into our films.

The year 1935 is often regarded as the starting-point in the development of a new type of music in pictures, for it was then that Arthur Bliss wrote his famous score for the H. G. Wells production *The Shape of Things to Come*. This was perhaps the first occasion on which a composer worked side by side with the film-makers from the scripting to the final editing. As Wells himself remarked : " The music is a part of the constructive scheme of the film, and the composer was practically a collaborator in its production. This Bliss music is not intended to be tacked on ; it is a part of the design." In the same year, William Walton wrote his first film score—for the Elizabeth Bergner picture *Escape Me Never*. William Alwyn wrote his first film music in 1936 for a documentary called *The Future's in the Air*; later films of his have included *Desert Victory*, *Odd Man Out*, *The October Man*, *Captain Boycott* and many other famous British movies. As the music of the screen progressed, a school of experts grew up between 1935 and 1939, among them Arthur Benjamin, John Greenwood, Mischa Spoliansky, Miklos Rozsa (now in Hollywood) and Richard Addinsell.

I think the war years, which gave far less drawing-room comedies and eternal-triangle melodramas, made for a more serious approach and widened the scope considerably. As a result most of the first-class contemporary composers in this country have now contributed to the cinema. In 1940, I was fortunate enough to be able to introduce Ralph Vaughan Williams to film music writing; this was for *49th Parallel* written at the age of 69 by the " grand old man of English music " as Vaughan Williams is often called. Coming into more recent times, Arthur Bliss wrote the music for *Men of Two Worlds*, John Ireland scored *The Overlanders* and Benjamin Britten composed the music for *Instruments of the Orchestra*.

I would like now to consider briefly the work of just two of the many composers whose work earned a comment Arthur Rank received while in America recently, to the effect that one of the things the American industry had been most impressed with was the quality and standard of performance of the music in our pictures. The films in question are two very famous ones: *Hamlet* and *Oliver Twist*. Much has been written about them, but I would like for a moment to look simply at one particular aspect of these two masterpieces—the music.

William Walton began his film career in 1935 with *Escape Me Never*, and in 1936, he wrote the music for his first Shakespearean production, *As You Like It*. In 1939, he returned again for another Bergner film *Stolen Life*, followed by *Major Barbara* in 1941, and *Next of Kin*, *The Foreman Went to France*, *Went the Day Well?* and *First of the Few* in 1942. In 1944, Laurence Olivier invited him to provide the music for his colour production of *Henry V*; the music was an outstanding success, receiving

many favourable comments from the film critics (who are normally "immune" to this question of music) and was recorded by H.M.V. on a set of four records. It was natural therefore that Walton should be called in again when the question of composition for *Hamlet* was raised, and the result has again proved very satisfactory. Let me give you a single example (which you can examine for yourself at the cinema) to show how musical effects are planned for a film and how they are recorded. The example in question is the famous Players' Scene. The Court arrive in the Council Chamber for the play and are greeted by Hamlet. They take their places and the actors begin their story. But Hamlet has arranged that they shall do a play which re-enacts the true story of the poisoning of his father by the man who has usurped the throne—his brother, who, as King, sits with his Queen to witness the entertainment. The play however has such an effect on the King that he eventually can stand it no longer and flees from the hall in a great rage. The whole of the play-acting is done in mime, so there was practically no dialogue to consider and the music had to be designed so that it could carry much of the effective-ness of the scene. This is how it was done.

The arrival of the Court is heralded by trumpet calls and a superb march theme which appears to keep step with the retinue as they take their places around the King's dais. Then the players make their entry, accompanied by a small group of musicians. For this, Walton used an orchestra of two violas, 'cello, oboe, cor anglais, bassoon and

Recording William Walton's music for Hamlet; *a general impres-sion of the Music Recording Theatre at Denham.*

harpsichord. To accompany the commencement of the play itself, we hear a sarabande in slow three-in-a-measure dance time, followed by a slower, sinister passage for the entry of the poisoner. As the camera moves round to show the reactions of the audience, and particularly of the King, the lightly-orchestrated stage music dissolves into angry mutterings from a full symphony orchestra, expressive of the underlying unrest and tension in the Court.

The camera, from its circular tracking orbit, returns to the play actors, and the music reverts to the quiet accompaniment of the small band. The actor-king has been poisoned and his murderer gains the favour of his widow with costly gifts. The King can stand the strain no longer (" The play's the thing wherein I'll catch the conscience of the King.") The full power of the orchestra rises up, swamping the soft sounds of the 'cello, oboe and harpsichord, and ends in a tremendous chord, as the King roars out " Give me some Light ! "

When you see *Hamlet* again (and I hope you will see it more than once, for such a film fully deserves more than one viewing) notice yourself how carefully Walton planned this little section, just one of many similar scenes in the picture in which the music was able to give added drama and excitement.

In 1943, Sir Arnold Bax, Master of the King's Musick, and the composer of the fanfares for the Royal Wedding and music for other State occasions, wrote his first film music for *Malta G.C.*, a documentary picture. In 1948, he made his first contribution to feature films when he worked with Ronald Neame and David Lean on *Oliver Twist*. As with *Hamlet*, I was the Music Director and had the pleasure of recording the music with the Philharmonia Orchestra, one of Britain's leading symphony orchestras. Sir Arnold wrote his score down in Sussex at the delightful country hotel where he lives, and I used to pay him regular visits during the ten weeks he was engaged in producing the music after he had seen the film twice in its entirety at Pinewood Studios. When the music had been completed and recorded, we were able to prepare a delightful orchestral suite

Recording session group : Muir Mathieson, William Walton, E. A. Drake (Music Recordist) and Laurence Olivier (left to right) photographed during the recording of music for Hamlet.

from the material used, recalling many of the fascinating moments from the picture. The scene in which Oliver asks for more, for example, is neatly outlined by the orchestra ; after Oliver has said, " Please, sir, I want some more," the three startled " whats " that follow are punctuated by staccato chords on full orchestra. The Chairman's remark " asked for more " is also followed up by a chord, which leads into a musical comment as a notice is displayed outside the workhouse advising the offer of the rebellious boy to anyone who will take him in.

During the last ten or fifteen years, I have had the interesting task of introducing many of our leading composers to the film studio. Men whose names are famous throughout the world wherever contemporary music is listened to and discussed have not only shown an intense interest in the new medium of expression, but have also demonstrated a firm technical grasp of the specialised work involved in film music. At the same time, we have established a group of specialists in film composition who spend a large amount of their time in experimenting and examining all the possibilities offered by the cinema. Our plan is that British films should not only have the best actors and actresses, the best directors, the best story writers and the best photographers, but also the best music it is possible to obtain, in order that your film-going may be enhanced by good listening as well as good looking and that our sound-tracks should be worthy of the finest traditions of film-making the world can offer.

MUIR MATHIESON, Denham, 1948.

Mr. and Mrs. Thin Man—the lovely and eternally youthful MYRNA LOY with suave WILLIAM POWELL, one of the most consistently entertaining acting combinations of the screen.

GENERAL *The* RELEASES
of the year, in pictures
1948

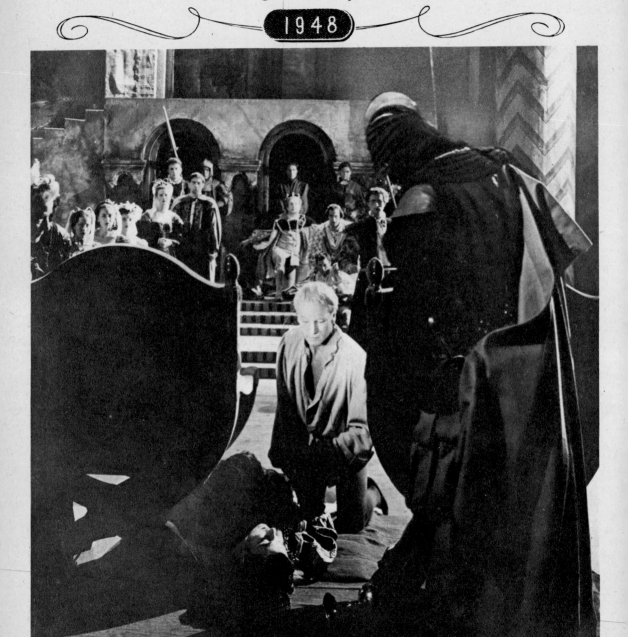

Most expensive, ambitious, interesting and in many ways the most successful British film of 1948, HAMLET earned for its producer-director-star LAURENCE OLIVIER, as well as for the British film industry in general, fresh laurels and prestige. Here Olivier is seen bidding farewell to his self-poisoned Queen mother (EILEEN HERLIE), while his stepfather king (BASIL SYDNEY), friend Horatio (NORMAN WOOLAND, extreme right) and the courtiers look on.

Convinced that the king has murdered his father, Hamlet (OLIVIER) draws his dagger and prepares to mete out justice while the conscience-stricken man says his prayers. But he hesitates—and forever is lost.

JEAN SIMMONS had the chance of her young career when Olivier chose her to play Ophelia in his film. She brought to the screen a new and more simple conception of the role, so made it all the more natural and moving.

A tense moment for Bob Hope and Bing Crosby in their 1948 addition to the famous *Paramount* Road series—ROAD TO RIO. Inset : the vaudeville team of Hope and Crosby put across their act.

LARRY PARKS as a young Scots chieftain who falls in love with the daughter of the chief of a rival clan (the daughter being lovely ELLEN DREW) in *Columbia's* Technicolored THE SWORDSMAN.

The 1947/48 Charles Chaplin film, MONSIEUR VERDOUX (sub-titled A Comedy of Murders) caused quite a controversy, some disliking the humour obtained from the sombre theme of a man marrying and murdering as a career. But it was quite undeniably a brilliant movie, mixing satire and slapstick, with a few more moving scenes sandwiched in between.

Honest, struggling young doctor (new star MICHAEL DENISON) tells his poor patient Lily (JOSEPHINE STUART) that she needs a good meal more than she needs the medicine his wife (DULCIE GRAY) is handing her in this scene from the excellent *Associated British* picture MY BROTHER JONATHAN.

A refugee from domestic worries, the Judge (ALEXANDER KNOX) settles down in his new job as snack-bar cook. Looking on is GEORGE TOBIAS and ANN SOTHERN. *R.K.O. Radio's* delightful INDIAN SUMMER.

ANN SHERIDAN, suspected of killing her former lover, visits the District Attorney. While friend and legal adviser LEW AYRES explains the complicated circumstances of the crime, husband ZACHARY SCOTT is surprised at evidence he knows nothing about. *Warner's* interesting film about marital infidelity, THE UNFAITHFUL.

Lord Goring (MICHAEL WILDING) congratulates Mrs. Cheveley (PAULETTE GODDARD) for her good sense in handing over the letter she has been trying to blackmail him with. A scene from *Korda's* superbly Technicolored, lavish film of the Oscar Wilde play AN IDEAL HUSBAND.

VALERIE HOBSON as the ambitious Blanche of the title in *Cineguild's* Technicolored film version of the Joseph Shearing period novel BLANCHE FURY.

29

One of the outstanding British films of the year was *Ealing's* brilliant IT ALWAYS RAINS ON SUNDAY, a finely perceptive picture of London life as lived down Bethnal Green way. Here is the Sandigate family after Sunday lunch—GOOGIE WITHERS, PATRICIA PLUNKETT, EDWARD CHAPMAN, DAVID LINES and SUSAN SHAW. Inset: Drama enters when an old boy-friend (JOHN McCALLUM) of the wife (GOOGIE WITHERS) arrives at the house and demands shelter.

Detective ROBERT YOUNG questions suspect killer ROBERT RYAN in Hollywood's first film to tackle the Anti-Semitic question; *R.K.O. Radio's* CROSSFIRE. Inset: Young questions GLORIA GRAHAME about the murder of the jew.

Mentally tortured JOAN CRAWFORD introduces the man she loves (VAN HEFLIN) to her new husband (RAYMOND MASSEY) in *Warner's* thoughtful drama POSSESSED, which gave Miss Crawford another opportunity for a fine performance.

ERIC PORTMAN watches with cynical amusement admirer DERMOT WALSH say good-night to the woman (his brother's wife, SALLY GRAY) he ruthlessly plans to make his own. The *Two Cities* film THE MARK OF CAIN.

Blanche Fury (VALERIE HOBSON) realises that the love which has blazed up between herself and Philip Thorn (STEWART GRANGER) can have no future for either of them while her husband lives. A scene from the superbly Techni-colored *Cineguild* dramatisation of the melodramatic BLANCHE FURY.

One of the most polished actors on the screen is GEORGE SANDERS, good in everything he does. Here he is with co-star ANGELA LANSBURY in a scene from *M.G.M's* THE AFFAIRS OF BEL AMI.

Sincere lay-psychiatrist BURGESS MEREDITH makes a last effort to save his suicidal patient KIERON MOORE in Anthony Kimmins' extremely intelligent and generally excellent MINE OWN EXECUTIONER.

The saboteur gang, now finally trained and ready for action, listen to last-minute instructions from their chief (JAMES ROBERTSON JUSTICE, standing) in *Ealing's* drama of the Belgian underground—AGAINST THE WIND. Left to right: GORDON JACKSON, SIMONE SIGNORET, JOHN SLATER, JACK WARNER. Inset: A traitor (JACK WARNER) is discovered.

A family scene from *Sydney Box's* amusing comedy about Football Pools, EASY MONEY, which in several episodes showed how the money was won and what happens to the people who win it: Grandma (MABEL CONSTANDUROS), mother (MARJORIE FIELDING), Jackie (PETULA CLARK) and father (JACK WARNER). Inset (top): Double bass player EDWARD RIGBY tells fellow musician GUY ROLFE what he will do with his windfall. (Left): Cabaret singer GRETA GYNT persuades Pools worker DENNIS PRICE to try a little crookery.

The Brighton Racecourse gang, led by boy murderer Pinkie (RICHARD ATTENBOROUGH, on bed), discuss their next move. Left to right: NIGEL STOCK, WYLIE WATSON, WILLIAM HARTNELL. The Boulting Brothers' film of the Graham Greene book and play BRIGHTON ROCK. Inset: Pinkie with the 17-year-old girl he marries and then tries to murder (" discovery " CAROL MARSH).

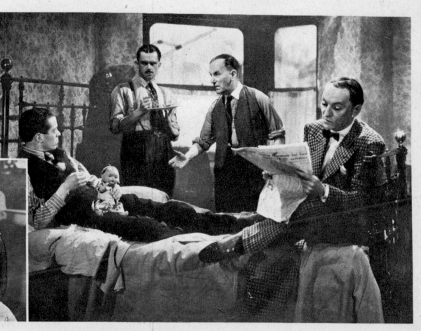

Paramount's new and popular star LIZABETH SCOTT has been seen in several of the year's releases.

36

MAXWELL REED shows his strangely sexed girl-friend (SIOBHAN MCKENNA) what she did to him at their last meeting. *Alliance's* DAUGHTER OF DARKNESS.

Hotel clerk MIKHAIL RASUMNY explains to air crew WALLY CASSELL, ALAN LADD and DOUGLAS DICK how difficult it is to find room for VERONICA LAKE. *Paramount's* SAIGON.

Robert (GEORGE SANDERS) follows Sandra (LUCILLE BALL) into the kitchen to the surprise of Maxwell (ALAN MOWBRAY) and the maid (EUNICE RUSSELL). Hunt Stromberg's PERSONAL COLUMN.

Suave crook KIRK DOUGLAS points the business end of his revolver towards the pal he has double-crossed (BURT LANCASTER) and the girl he has disgusted (LIZABETH SCOTT). *Paramount's* grim I WALK ALONE.

At the tea for the elite of 1880 Paris, unscrupulous social climber GEORGE SANDERS gets close to ANN DVORAK and ANGELA LANSBURY, the first two of the six romances which help pave his way to success in the *Loew-Lewin* production of De Maupassant's THE AFFAIRS OF BEL AMI.

BARBARA STANWYCK and ERROL FLYNN lock down at the body of the former's husband in *Warner's* mystery-thriller CRY WOLF.

Sydney Box took Peter Blackmore's fairly successful play about a Mermaid, MIRANDA, and turned it into a delightful comedy movie. As the man-hungry lady-with-a-tail, GLYNIS JOHNS gave a grand performance, while GRIFFITH JONES (seen here with her) as the young doctor who takes her home to his wife as a holiday memento was equally excellent. Inset: And so we leave Miranda—with *her* memento of an "interesting" episode on dry land.

One of the strangest, in many ways most hauntingly beautiful, British pictures of the year was the Rudolph Cartier-Edana Romney production for *J. Arthur Rank*, CORRIDOR OF MIRRORS, which introduced, opposite ERIC PORTMAN, a lovely newcomer in South African-born EDANA ROMNEY. Miss Romney also collaborated on the screenplay.

A scene from Cecil B. de Mille's typically lavish, brightly Technicolored slice of American history, UNCONQUERED. Star GARY COOPER is seated at the table (third sitting figure from the right).

One of the more interesting, adult (though often terribly confusing) movies of 1948 was the ORSON WELLES thriller for *Columbia,* LADY FROM SHANGHAI, in which he not only starred but also directed and produced his own screenplay. With him were his (then) wife RITA HAYWORTH and two out-outstanding new players in EVERETT SLOANE (seen here with Welles in the amazing Court-room scene) and GLENN ANDERS.

Escaped convict HUMPHREY BOGART (unjustly convicted of wife-murder) looks at the face the plastic surgeon has given him while the girl who befriends him in his flight (LAUREN BACALL) watches him. A scene from *Warner's* thriller DARK PASSAGE.

42

One of the best—and most successful—American films for years has been Samuel Goldwyn's THE BEST YEARS OF OUR LIVES, which in America last year monotonously won nearly every prize it could be entered for. More realistically than any previous movie, it showed the reactions of the soldiers returning to Civvy Street. Here is father FREDRIC MARCH, with wife MYRNA LOY and daughter TERESA WRIGHT.

KAY WALSH, in taffeta and lace, in the Peter Ustinov film of the F. Anstey farce
VICE VERSA—A *Two Cities* picture.

44

Happy end to a charming adventure. The lost British girl (PATRICIA ROC), her enthusiastic but unfortunate Italian suitor (BONAR COLLEANO), the film director (CHARLES GOLDNER) and the tenor-hero (NINO MARTINI) in the final scene of the gay, very pleasing *Two Cities* musical romance, ONE NIGHT WITH YOU. Inset: Stranded passengers ROC and MARTINI find they aren't going to get much help from station master RICHARD HEARNE.

Lovely Austrian Countess JOAN FONTAINE comes to beg the assistance of American phonograph salesman BING CROSBY—and brings a little force to her argument. A scene from *Paramount's* Technicolored musical THE EMPEROR WALTZ.

One of the most artistic, sincere and beautifully photographed movies of the year was John Ford's *R.K.O. Radio* picture THE FUGITIVE, made in Mexico. HENRY FONDA plays the priest who finds courage with his faith and dies proudly for it: J. CARROL NAISH is the informer who pleads for a blessing after for personal gain he has given the priest into the hands of the firing squad.

The amusing if seriously intended duel with whips, scene from Maurice Ostrer's IDOL OF PARIS. Whippers are CHRISTINE NORDEN (left) and BERYL BAXTER (right).

While the atmosphere between JOAN BENNETT and ROBERT RYAN becomes charged with electricity, Miss Bennett's artist-husband watches with sightless eyes. A scene from *R.K.O. Radio's* WOMAN ON THE BEACH.

One of the mobsters (WALTER CRISHAM) gets from his boss's (JACK LA RUE) gun what was coming to him, while the unfortunate Miss B. looks suitably astonished. A scene from NO ORCHIDS FOR MISS BLANDISH, a *Renown* production.

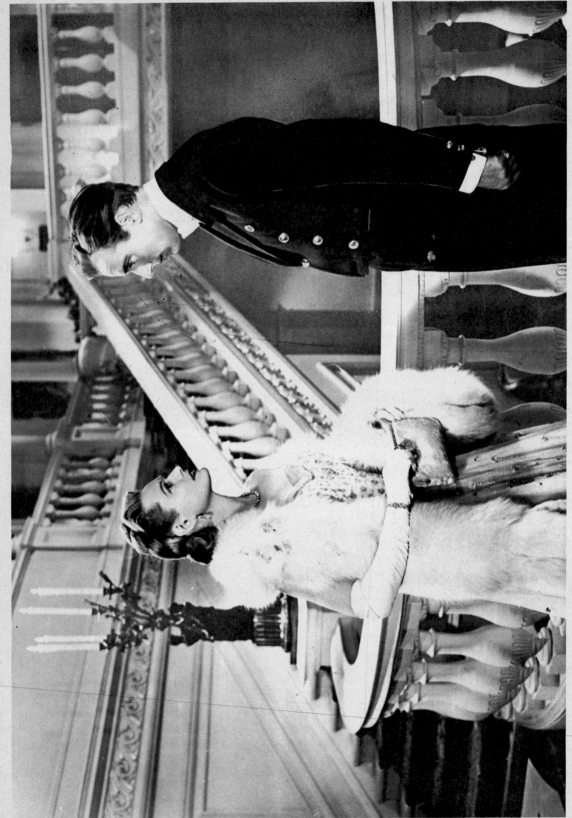

My Lady (ANNA NEAGLE) meets My Lord the Butler (MICHAEL WILDING) in the gay, carefree and altogether highly diverting Herbert Wilcox romantic comedy SPRING IN PARK LANE.—*British Lion.*

Alexander Korda's lavish, spectacular production of BONNIE PRINCE CHARLIE has had a somewhat uneven journey to the screen. Started more than a year ago, repeatedly held up, it has had three directors working on it at various times and even now may not be generally released until 1949, though it is scheduled for London premiere late in 1948. Not the least of the troubles was the death of Will Fyffe, who had an important part in the picture; because of this many sequences had to be shot all over again. But now, at last, with Anthony Kimmins in control of the direction, BONNIE PRINCE CHARLIE is finished. This picture is of David Niven, in completely authentic period dress, who plays the title role.

Lover, wife and husband : KIERON MOORE shields VIVIEN LEIGH from the ire of RALPH RICHARDSON, a scene from another lavish Korda production, ANNA KARENINA, based on the famous Tolstoy tragedy. A further scene from this important 1948 production will be found on the next page.

The English Screen offered many fine acting performances during the year, but few finer than that of RALPH RICHARDSON, playing the ill-used Karenin in Alexander Korda's, Julien Duvivier directed, production of the Leo Tolstoy novel ANNA KARENINA. With Richardson in this picture is his wife, played by VIVIEN LEIGH.

50

Starry get-together in the David O. Selznick production of THE PARADINE CASE, directed by Alfred Hitchcock. In this scene the case is being discussed by (left to right) ANN TODD, JOAN TETZEL, GREGORY PECK, ETHEL BARRYMORE, CHARLES COBURN and CHARLES LAUGHTON, and being discussed with such obvious interest that the after-dinner coffee remains untouched. Inset: Mrs. Paradine, played by lovely Italian actress VALLI, is helped into her coat before being arrested, charged with the murder of her husband, about which THE PARADINE CASE is concerned.

New British Discovery DIRK BOGARDE, playing William Latch, faces his mother (MARY CLARE) who obviously disapproves of him taking the position of footman in the household. But Esther (KATHLEEN RYAN) just as obviously holds a reverse opinion! A scene from the *Wessex* production ESTHER WATERS.

Sydney Box's JOURNEY INTO YESTERDAY was a film about Displaced Persons and a number of diverse nationalities are represented in this scene, where British Major Lawrence, GUY ROLFE, questions Hildegard (MAI ZETTERLING) seated. Tensely interested, surrounding group includes GERARD HEINZ, HERBERT LOM, SYBILLA BINDER and PATRICK HOLT.

Every Launder and Gilliat (*Individual Productions*) movie has been outstanding, largely due to first-class script and superb dialogue. LONDON BELONGS TO ME, their 1948 offering, was no exception. Scene here, an awkward moment, includes (left to right) WYLIE WATSON, FAY COMPTON, new star SUSAN SHAW and ANDREW CRAWFORD.

Romance at the rail; GEORGE BRENT meets glamorous FRANCES GIFFORD on deck in this scene from the *Metro-Goldwyn-Mayer* Technicolor musical LUXURY LINER which will be a 1949 release.

Fashion designer JOAN CRAW-FORD rather too conscientiously studies her brush while DANA ANDREWS contemptuously watches her and MARTHA STEWART interestedly watches *him*. A scene from 20th *Century-Fox's* DAISY KENYON.

Caught in the act: PAULETTE GODDARD and MACDONALD CAREY in an amusing scene from *Paramount's* HAZARD.

Authenticity in the court case that is the high spot of the *Gainsborough* film THE BLIND GODDESS is guaranteed by the fact that it was authored by the famous K.C., Sir Patrick Hastings. Scene here introduces (left to right) CLIVE MORTON, HUGH WIL-LIAMS, ANNE CRAWFORD and ERIC PORTMAN.

The three partners in crime (ALEC GUINNESS, ROBERT NEWTON and KAY WALSH, playing Fagin, Bill Sykes and Nancy) discuss their plot in the ill-famed Three Cripples Tavern. A scene from *Cineguild's* OLIVER TWIST, which many people, including the writer, rank as the best British film of 1948.

Inset 1 (*left*): Later in a fit of drunken rage, Sykes kills Nancy. Inset 2 (*right*): Oliver Twist (JOHN HOWARD DAVIES) runs in terror from his pursuers.

More than somewhat tropical is this scene shared by ESTHER WILLIAMS and PETER LAWFORD in the aptly titled *Metro-Goldwyn-Mayer* Technicolored musical ON AN ISLAND WITH YOU. At the time of writing this picture is scheduled for 1949 release.

Anthony Havelock-Allen, formerly with *Cineguild*, this year broke away to form his own production unit, *Constellation Films*. First movie, THE SMALL VOICE, starred Mrs. Havelock-Allen (VALERIE HOBSON, second from left). Also in this scene are HAROLD KEEL and JAMES DONALD.

JOAN CAULFIELD looks down at inanimate AUDREY TOTTER while CLAUDE RAINS phones for the police and MICHAEL NORTH looks hopelessly on, a tense moment from *Warner's* thriller THE UNSUSPECTED.

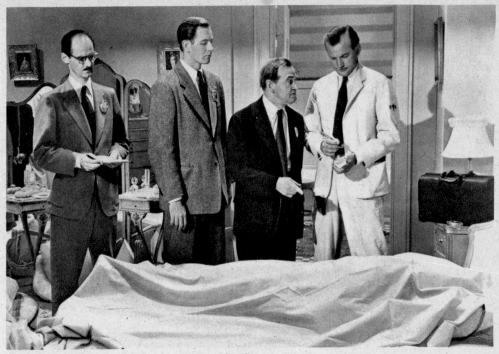

When famous New York columnist and film producer Mark Hellinger made THE
NAKED CITY for *Universal-International* he went out and shot his film, a whodunnit,
against a background of the actual streets and buildings of New York. Here detective
BARRY FITZGERALD and young assistant DON TAYLOR (centre) discuss with the doctors
the cause of death.

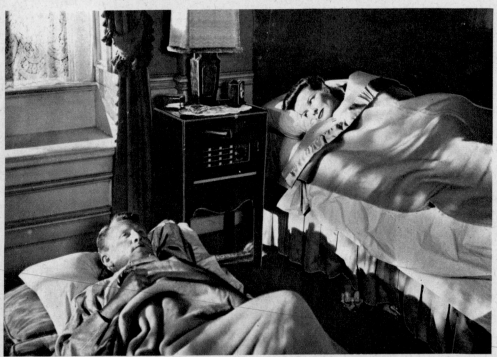

SPENCER TRACY discovers that his 'state of union' with wife KATHARINE HEPBURN is far more
unsatisfactory that his 'state of union' with the nation's political leaders. A scene from
the *Metro-Goldwyn-Mayer* picture, THE WORLD AND HIS WIFE (titled STATE
OF THE UNION in America).

An unpleasant moment in a restaurant when a drunken diner starts to pass remarks about "Jews in uniform". A scene from *20th Century-Fox's* "Oscar"-winning film on the theme of anti-Semitism, GENTLEMAN'S AGREEMENT. Crusading journalist GREGORY PECK watches his Jewish officer-friend JOHN GARFIELD react to the sneer. Inset: A happier moment, with GARFIELD, PECK, DOROTHY McGUIRE and CELESTE HOLM.

GREGORY PECK and new Italian star VALLI in the Alfred Hitchcock directed, David O.
Selznick production THE PARADINE CASE.

ANN SHERIDAN and ERROL FLYNN assist THOMAS MITCHELL in this scene from the *Warner* Western SILVER RIVER.

LILLI PALMER leans over the banisters to talk to her co-star, newcomer SAM WANAMAKER, in the *Warner* picture MY GIRL TISA.

A more grown-up SHIRLEY TEMPLE was revealed in *Warner's* THAT HAGEN GIRL. Here she is with co-star RONALD REAGAN.

Gainsborough's QUARTETTE was an interesting production in that it took four short stories by Somerset Maugham and combined them into one film. Illustration (A) is from the "Alien Corn" episode; it shows DIRK BOGARDE confessing to HONOR BLACKMAN that in spite of two years spent studying in Paris his piano playing is still not up to standard. Second illustration (B) shows JACK WATLING having

beginner's luck at Monte Carlo in "The Facts of Life" episode: leaning over his shoulder is MAI ZETTERLING. The last illustration (C) is from the episode called "The Kite" and shows SUSAN SHAW knocking a cup of tea into GEORGE COLE'S lap during an exciting moment in the film.

DENNIS MORGAN'S hand steals toward his hidden gun while being held up by desperate outlaw ARTHUR KENNEDY. Obviously wondering whether he'll make it is JANE WYMAN. *Warners'*
CHEYENNE was one of the simpler but better Westerns of the year.

Thanks to an outstanding comedy performance by CLIFTON WEBB (right), playing the most
unconventional baby-minder there ever was, 20th *Century-Fox's* SITTING PRETTY
emerged as one of the most consistently funny pictures of the year. Also in the picture
are Mr. Webb's employers, MAUREEN O'HARA and ROBERT YOUNG.

Dainty little ballerina MARGARET O'BRIEN in *Metro-Goldwyn-Mayer's* Technicolored story of the ballet, THE UNFINISHED DANCE.

Amber (LINDA DARNELL) goes to the side of her lover (CORNEL WILDE) when the former is challenged by her "protector" (GLENN LANGAN) to a duel to the death. *20th Century-Fox's* Technicolored adaptation of the Kathleen Winsor novel, FOREVER AMBER.

The unfortunate missionary's widow (ANN TODD) poses for the unmoral and crooked artist (RAY MILLAND) in the *Paramount British* period piece SO EVIL MY LOVE.

First movie to be directed by Robert Montgomery since his sensationally good LADY IN THE LAKE was *Universal-International's* crime thriller RIDE THE PINK HORSE. WANDA HENDRIX leans over MONTGOMERY after the latter has been stabbed in the back by thugs.

Quite a lot of moviegoers found *R.K.O. Radio's* THE BISHOP'S WIFE to be one of the year's funnier comedies. In it Bishop DAVID NIVEN (inset) prays for help and gets Angel CARY GRANT— seen here with Mrs. " Bishop " (LORETTA YOUNG) and family friend (MONTY WOOLLEY).

With gun at the ready VICTOR MATURE makes his escape up the stairs in the 20th Century-Fox Western, FURY AT FURNACE CREEK.

Having sawn through his own half of the hand-cuffs, callous escapee JACK WARNER now tells his terrified younger companion in crime, GEORGE COLE, that from now on he is on his own—Sydney Box's *Gainsborough* production MY BROTHER'S KEEPER.

LANA TURNER played a nurse and CLARK GABLE a doctor in *Metro-Goldwyn-Mayer's* drama of wartime marital complications HOMECOMING.

Many of those " in the know " have tipped IRENE DUNNE as the most likely winner of next year's Oscar for her altogether charming performance in the *R.K.O. Radio* picture I REMEMBER MAMA. Holding her hand is daughter BARBARA BEL GEDDES : behind her is husband PHILIP DORN.

One of busy MARGARET LOCKWOOD's 1948 films was the *Corfield-Huth* production, LOOK BEFORE YOU LOVE, in which she co-stars with GRIFFITH JONES.

STEWART GRANGER in *Two Cities'* WOMAN HATER invites a Continental film star (EDWIGE FEUILLERE) to his home to find out if her reputation of hating men is true. He tries to warm her with a glass of brandy, but ends in warming himself a little too much!

Looking incredibly young and wistful, JOAN FONTAINE resists her friend's (CAROL YORKE'S) efforts to question her about a boy friend—from *Universal-International's* LETTER FROM AN UNKNOWN WOMAN.

GREER GARSON shares starring honours with ROBERT MITCHUM and new star RICHARD HART (not in picture) in *Metro-Goldwyn-Mayer's* DESIRE ME (former title A WOMAN OF MY OWN).

When PHYLLIS CALVERT went across to America on a kind of filmic reverse lend-lease mission for Mr. Rank, she made for *Paramount* a picture called MY OWN TRUE LOVE, in which she co-starred with MELVYN DOUGLAS. In this intimate scene the two share an early cup of coffee.

Neither WILLIAM POWELL, IRENE DUNNE nor ZASU PITTS make many appearances on the screen these days; therefore their work together in *Warners'* wonderful period comedy LIFE WITH FATHER was all the more welcome. With the trio here is (side view) EDMUND GWENN.

THE SAINTED SISTERS of the title in the *Paramount* picture are JOAN CAULFIELD and VERONICA LAKE, seen here with BARRY FITZGERALD (to their left) and BEULAH BONDI (extreme left).

Killer McCoy MICKEY ROONEY begins to wonder who kills and who gets killed in this ringside, between-rounds moment from the *Metro-Goldwyn-Mayer* film KILLER McCOY. With him are trainer SAM LEVENE and manager BRIAN DONLEVY.

BOND STREET, Anatole de Grunwald's *Pathe* production, was a movie with several varying episodes. One of these concerned an escaped gangster (DEREK FARR) and the girl (JEAN KENT) he picks up and then callously double-crosses.

ALAN LADD and BRENDA MARSHALL in a scene from *Paramount's* WHISPERING SMITH, with Ladd playing a two-gun railway detective of the 1890's and Brenda as his best friend's wife.

Sydney Box's GOOD TIME GIRL was concerned with the problem of wayward youth and its drift into crime. An excellent movie, its cast included GRIFFITH JONES (a smart racketeer) and JEAN KENT (the girl who drifts into crime through an initial double-cross and unfair reformatory sentence).

Right : Sydney Box's DAYBREAK was a gloomy little story about a hangman (ERIC PORTMAN) who marries a charming little waterside waif (ANN TODD) without telling her of his " sideline "—a deception that leads to final tragedy.

Left : First post-tax American film to reach this country was *Metro-Goldwyn-Mayer's* THE BRIDE GOES WILD, a gay and laughable comedy with VAN JOHNSON, JUNE ALLYSON and JACKIE (" Butch ") JENKINS.

John Lund, Gail Russell and Edward G. Robinson share an exciting moment from *Paramount's* THE NIGHT HAS A THOUSAND EYES, a thriller.

When *Two Cities* decided to re-make that thriller success of yesteryear, *Rome Express*, they asked John Paddy Carstairs to direct it with the new title of SLEEPING CAR TO TRIESTE. An all-star cast includes Albert Lieven, Jean Kent and Dino Galvani.

Metro-Goldwyn-Mayer's BODY AND SOUL was another story of the boxing ring, but extremely well done and therefore excellently entertaining. Here is John Garfield as the East Side boy who fights his way to the world championships, mother (Ann Revere) and girl-friend (Lilli Palmer).

Frank Sinatra and a somewhat more than thinly disguised J. Carrol Naish in *Metro-Goldwyn-Mayer's* Technicolored, Joe Pasternak production, THE KISSING BANDIT—a 1949 release.

The Girl (PEGGY CUMMINS) finds the Fugitive (REX HARRISON); a scene from 20th Century-Fox's British production ESCAPE, based on the Galsworthy novel.

JEAN PIERRE AUMONT as successful suitor for the hand of Princess Charlotte (newcomer JOAN HOPKINS) while the Prince Regent (CECIL PARKER) tries to make the best of his defeat. Columbia's British film of the Norman Ginsbury play THE FIRST GENTLE-MAN.

The passengers of the wrecked Dakota begin to realise what they are in for: DAVID TOM-LINSON, boxing champion ANDREW CRAWFORD, manager CHARLES VICTOR and air hostess PHYLLIS CALVERT in a scene from the Box-Gainsborough production BROKEN JOURNEY.

RONALD COLMAN meets the little cafe waitress (SHELLEY WINTERS) for the first time. Later, when his role of Othello has driven him nearly mad, he ... his ... the ... able final tragedy. A scene from Universal-International's A DOUBLE LIFE.

THE YEAR IN DISNEY LAND

As this particular section of *Film Review* goes to press (and, rather unfortunately in the circumstances, it happens to be one of the earliest) neither Walt Disney nor distributors R.K.O. Radio have any idea whether the maestro's only new full-length effort, *Melody Time*, is likely to be released, or even premiered, in England this year, or whether we shall have to wait until early 1949 to see it.
In any case, no stills or pictorial matter of any kind are available at this moment to give you a pre-view of the kind of picture it is. So I thought, in the circumstances, the only alternative—other than ignoring an important cinematic event—was to ask Disney to himself describe his production. And this is what he has done for you on this page. Should later news come in about the release of *Melody Time* before the last section of this volume goes to press, I shall give it somewhere in the Stop Press pages at the end.
The Editor

SOME FACTS ABOUT *MELODY TIME* by WALT DISNEY

AN important period in the history of the Disney product will be marked by the release of our new feature-length fantasy *Melody Time*, and, since it may seem to signalize a departure from such productions as *Snow White and the Seven Dwarfs*, *Pinocchio*, *Dumbo* and *Bambi* and, other similar features already announced for our forthcoming programme, our new filmusical prompts an explanation as to its origin and technique.

In the first place I want to stress that the multiple-episode cartoon fantasy will not replace the classic fable picture on the Disney schedule. From our standpoint the *Melody Time* formula is as essentially " Disney " as any other kind of screen entertainment associated with our name, the one type merely offering a change of pace from the other, and keeping our products from crystallizing around a set specification.

The literary archives of the world are filled with screenable riches, with tale and anecdote, fable and fantastic folklore. Wonderfully amusing and dramatically potent, they are often so concentrated in form as to be entirely unsuited for feature-length film treatment.

After the war, when once again we could think about entertainment films, we had in mind a number of these titles such as " Peter and the Wolf " and " The Whale Who Wanted to Sing at the Met " which we were eager to make, but which didn't seem to fit into the usual screen pattern. Urged on by the times and circumstances we decided to assemble several of these in a novel presentation, and *Make Mine Music*, the finished product of our initial experiment, showed us we had discovered something very important for our bill of fare.

By all the evidence we were convinced that we had enlisted a new segment of habitual movie-goers, and we now know that the variety of important names from screen, radio and the realms of music who have enthusiastically adapted their gifts to our cartoons have proved a definite asset in enlarging our younger audience.

We followed up with *Fun and Fancy Free*, a combination of two distinct tales, and our latest feature along these lines has seven episodes woven around the core of American mythology.

Take, for example, the legendary figures of Pecos Bill, tall-tale hero of the cowboys, and Johnny Appleseed, the more modest but nevertheless colourful frontiersman, central characters in *Melody Time*. These two mighty men of folklore are a compound of anecdotes and prodigious deeds, but neither of them has more than the most sketchy " life story " with which to occupy the full seventy minutes of the feature picture. Yet, by letting them share time and honours with other cartoon performers, together with the living actors who sing and speak through the animations, we are able to keep them vividly alive for all kinds of audiences each and every moment they are on the screen.

On the basis of advance tests and polls for this our " myth-musical " we are confidently proceeding with another combination of fantasy in *Two Fabulous Characters*, wherein Ichabod Crane from " The Legend of Sleepy Hollow " will cavort with Mr. Toad from Kenneth Grahame's " Wind in the Willows."

Again I want to emphasize that the effective use of material otherwise denied to the motion picture is what appeals to me chiefly in making the kind of entertainment represented by *Melody Time*.

Ordinarily, changes in form and material come slowly in popular diversion, this applying to screen and stage alike, but occasionally there are circumstances which dictate swift innovation, and then we discover, to our amazement, that the public has been ready and waiting for some recipe we have been too timid to propose.

It pleases and encourages me to learn that the " Disney " style is not so fixed and limited in the public mind as to preclude further exploration in the field of entertainment.

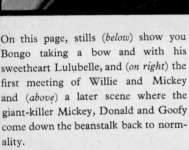

FUN AND FANCY FREE

On the previous page I have noted that it is doubtful whether the latest Walt Disney feature, *Melody Time*, will be seen in Britain before early 1949. But even if this is the case, the tax did not stop us from seeing at least one Disney full-length picture during the year, *Fun and Fancy Free*, released in February.

This two-part picture was firstly concerned with the adventures of Bongo, the performing bear who escapes from a circus and finds adventure and romance, and secondly with Mickey as a new kind of Jack the Giant Killer. This section of the picture served to introduce one of Disney's happiest creations for a long time, in Willie, the silly giant.

On this page, stills (*below*) show you Bongo taking a bow and with his sweetheart Lulubelle, and (*on right*) the first meeting of Willie and Mickey and (*above*) a later scene where the giant-killer Mickey, Donald and Goofy come down the beanstalk back to normality.

SOME OF THE YEAR'S "SHORTS"

Donald attempts to give his adopted orphan, a little Kangaroo, a bath in DADDY DUCK.

One of the more riotous of the many amusing moments in CLOWN OF THE JUNGLE, which introduced an irrepressible new character.

Another new 1948 Disney character is BOOTLE BEETLE, a rare kind of bug who turns out to be an adventurer at heart.

Donald's always precarious good humour is tried to the utmost when he crosses swords—and everything else handy—with a couple of chipmunks CHIP AN' DALE.

Sahara tourists Donald Duck and Goofy discover that they have run out of petrol in CRAZY WITH THE HEAT.

Pluto struggles on through snow and ice to deliver the mail on time in his new job of MAIL DOG.

Left.—Elephant-minder Goofy relaxes after giving his charge its weekly bath in THE BIG WASH.

Right.—Driven out of his home by the unaccountable behaviour of its plumbing, Donald tries to get a little cold comfort in DRIP DIPPY DONALD.

Goofy shows you how not to go hunting in the Disney short FOUL HUNTING. Only thing hurt is the hunter's pride.

Some uproarious fun with amateur punter Goofy in the Disney satire on the " Sport of Kings "—THEY'RE OFF.

Obviously Mickey has got the wrong impression about the egg in this sequence from Mickey's adventures in Australia—DOWN UNDER.

Donald gets hit on the head—which explains a lot of things about him, the examining psychiatrist tells Daisy Duck in DONALD'S DILEMMA.

CLARK GABLE co-starred with LANA TURNER for the third time in *Metro-Goldwyn-Mayer's* HOMECOMING, in which Gable plays a doctor who falls in love with nurse Lana.

The ADVANCE of COLOUR on the SCREEN

by

MARGARET ETTINGER,

Director of Public Relations for the
Technicolor Motion Picture Corporation

Dr. Herbert T. Kalmus, president of Technicolor Motion Picture Corporation, is a pioneer in the field of motion pictures in colour.

He prepared himself for a career as chemical engineer, graduating from Massachusetts Institute of Technology in 1904. He received a B.S. degree. Two years later he received the degree of Ph.D. at the University of Zurich, Switzerland.

Dr. Kalmus became president of Technicolor Motion Picture Corporation in 1916, serving in that capacity ever since. In 1922 he became president of Technicolor, Inc., which position he still holds.

Dr. Kalmus's first experimental work in motion pictures was done in 1912 on a device known as Vanascope, which he and his associates decided was impractical. Their interest in motion pictures aroused, they decided that pictures needed—and could be given—colour. Backed by Vanascope's principals, Dr. Kalmus and his associates went ahead with experiments and research. This work led to the formation of Technicolor, named as a tribute to the Massachusetts Institute of Technology.

The history of Technicolor under Dr. Kalmus is a record of continued research and experimentation which has led to the perfected three-colour process used on the screen today.

Dr. Kalmus was born in Chelsea, Massachusetts. His birthday is November 9th.

Dr. Herbert T. Kalmus, President and General Manager,
Technicolor Motion Picture Corporation

PROGRESS toward realization of the old dream of motion picture colour enthusiasts—an all-colour screen—has steadily continued, even in the face of hampering effects of the war and immediate post-war economic conditions.

According to present indications, the 1948 output of 35 mm. positive prints by Technicolor Motion Picture Corporation should set an all-time record.

The 1947 production was the highest to date—222,017,439 ft. In 1932 the production figure was 5,526,128. Thus the 35 mm. positive print output of Technicolor Motion Picture Corporation has increased more than 40-fold in the 15-year period.

In 1947 (for year ending Nov. 30), the 35 mm. positive print output of Technicolor Ltd., the British affiliated company, was 50,487,851 feet. This figure is more than nine times the total Technicolor production for 1932, when there was no British company.

Increase of Technicolor print output naturally is predicated upon the popularity of productions photographed in colour by Technicolor. Reports from distributors show that this popularity is on a world-wide scale.

Illustrative of this is the status of Technicolor pictures in Canada, England and the United States, from which countries accurate statistics are more easily obtainable. A few examples of exhibitor polls and box-office estimates made by publications of the motion picture industry may be cited.

The poll of U.S. exhibitors by *Showmen's Trade Review* on the ten top money-making pictures of 1947 placed seven productions photographed in colour by Technicolor, including first and second places.

The 1947 poll of Canadian theatremen on their ten best box-office attractions, conducted by the *Canadian Film Weekly*, gave place to six Technicolor productions. As in the American poll, Technicolor pictures captured first and second places.

Variety's listing of the "top grossers of 1947" on the basis of American and Canadian distributors' rental included 15 Technicolor productions in the first 25 pictures.

Motion Picture Herald listed nine pictures in the order of their box-office business in England in 1947. Three American-produced pictures won places in this category—all were Technicolor productions, as was one of the leading British-produced pictures.

Technicolor in 1947 enjoyed record production and record employment, according to the report of Technicolor, Inc., and subsidiary, Technicolor Motion Picture Corporation, by Dr. Herbert T. Kalmus, president and general manager, for the year ended Dec. 31, 1947. Capacity for service and product was sold out for the year 1948, it was stated.

During 1947, there were 30 feature-length productions photographed in colour by Technicolor Motion Picture Corporation in Hollywood. Six features were photographed by Technicolor Ltd., in England. The British company was photographing or preparing or had under contract nine feature pictures for 1948. The 1948 outlook for the American company was 48 productions being photographed, in preparation or under contract to be photographed.

For several years, both in the United States and England, the Technicolor plants have been unable to meet studio demand. This condition is due to World War II and post-war economic conditions. Technicolor had long-range plans for expansion of both plants as well as plans for eventual construction of laboratories in other countries. But these plans found themselves at the mercy of economic conditions, including the prime requisite of the availability of materials.

Production in both countries was stepped up, however, to the greatest extent that conditions would allow. In the United States, with studio demand already exceeding Technicolor capacity, the situation was further involved by the effect upon Technicolor Motion Picture Corporation of the protracted strike in the motion picture industry. For months laboratory facilities were affected, with a resultant delay in the production of release prints.

In his report for 1947, which was issued in March, 1948, Dr. Kalmus said it then appeared probable that Technicolor in Hollywood would reach a volume of approximately 320,000,000 feet a year of positive prints by the end of 1948 or early 1949.

The Technicolor expansion programme, he said, " despite strikes, shortage of materials, difficulty of obtaining permits, and other obstacles encountered, is well on its way." Additional negative storage vaults were being constructed at Van Nuys, Calif., near Hollywood, and buildings to house the rest of the machinery and equipment were being constructed in the block occupied by the present Technicolor plant in Hollywood.

" Some of the new machines are already installed and operating," he said. " A number of the existing ones have been improved and speeded up so that we are at present realizing over 40 per cent of the planned increases in services and product."

Increased capacity, Dr. Kalmus revealed, was not being used to offer customers more pictures in 1948 but to reduce the excessive backlog of print orders.

" In this way it is expected that the delay due to strikes and other causes which increased the elapsed time between completion of the photography of a feature production and the delivery of release prints will be reduced so that it will be steadily approaching normal during the year 1948.

" About September, 1948, we expect to begin to receive the new Technicolor three-strip cameras which are currently being built as a part of the expansion programme. At that time an increased volume of photography can be undertaken and as more cameras are delivered from that time on the volume of photography is expected to be correspondingly increased."

Illustrative of the growth of Technicolor, it may be recalled that the ancestor of the present Technicolor plants in Hollywood and London was a railway car. The first Technicolor laboratory was constructed in this car in Boston, and in 1917 was transported over the rails to Jacksonville, Fla., for the filming of the first Technicolor feature production, *The Gulf Between*. It had been preceded by one colour picture, produced in England by another process.

" We do not live in a black-and-white world, so our entertainment should not be in black-and-white."

This premise for the development of motion picture colour photography was laid down by Dr. Kalmus, who has been head of Technicolor since its inception, at the outset of his work in colour. In those pioneer days colour pictures were characterized by glaring hues and wide colour fringes— an object on the screen might have two outlines, one red, one green.

There was a premature rush to colour with Technicolor's two-component process in 1929 and 1930. Pictures were made in colour against the advice of Dr. Kalmus, who has persistently maintained :

" You cannot make a poor story good by sound, by colour or by any other device or embellishment. But you can make a good story better."

In 1932 Technicolor inaugurated its three-component process which is in current use. In addition, use is now being made of its monopack process, which does away with the necessity for special cameras.

The history of Technicolor has been one of continuous research and development. This is still going on.

High points in the development of Technicolor may be given as follows :

1917—THE GULF BETWEEN, first Technicolor feature.

1922—THE TOLL OF THE SEA, first production by two-component subtractive process.

1923—Establishment of first Technicolor laboratory in Hollywood.

1925—Douglas Fairbanks' THE BLACK PIRATE.

1928—THE VIKING, first Technicolor picture with music and sound effects.

1929—ON WITH THE SHOW, first all-talking Technicolor feature.

1932—FLOWERS AND TREES, first three-component Technicolor picture.

1936—Establishment of British Technicolor laboratory.

1938—SNOW WHITE AND THE SEVEN DWARFS, first Technicolor animated feature.

1939—GONE WITH THE WIND, greatest grossing feature in motion picture history.

1939—New Hollywood research laboratory and office building ; perfection of new Technicolor high speed film.

1940—Special award for Technicolor three-colour process by Academy of Motion Picture Arts and Sciences.

1944—THUNDERHEAD, first all-Monopack Technicolor feature.

1947—Record output of 35 mm. positive prints.

STAR PORTRAIT GALLERY

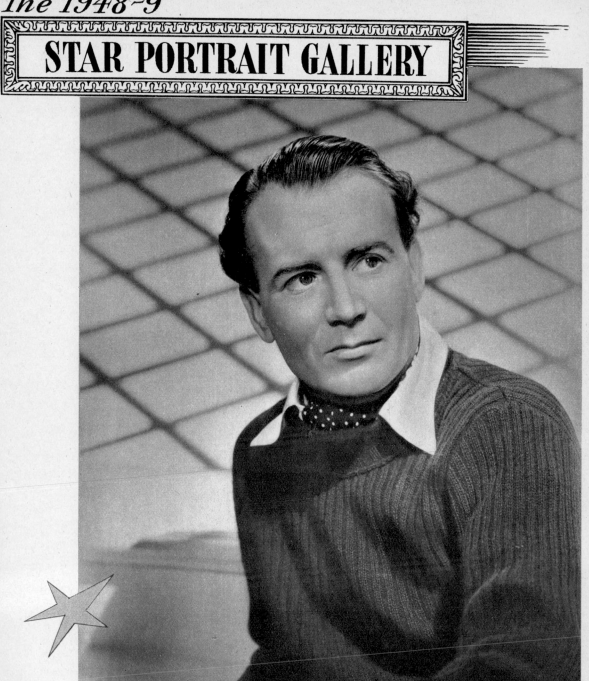

For JOHN MILLS this has been a great year. Not only did he become Britain's No. 1 film actor by winning the National Film Award, but he was also allowed for the first time to produce as well as star in a picture—a long-held ambition. Still under 40, married to successful playwright Mary Hayley-Bell and with one small daughter, Mills retains the appearance and the outlook of youth.

Vivacious *Paramount* starlet OLGA SAN JUAN.

MARGARET LOCKWOOD proved beyond all doubt her claim to be Britain's No. 1 film actress by this year, for the third time running, winning the annual *Daily Mail* Film Award with a clear margin of votes. Daughter of an engineer, Margaret was born in India in 1916, made her first stage appearance at the " Q " theatre in 1934. Her first film followed the same year (*Lorna Doone*, remember ?). Is married and has one adored small daughter, Margaret Junior.

Another man made happy by this year's *Daily Mail* poll was 35-year-old MICHAEL WILDING, who found himself elevated to second place in the male star list. Michael celebrated his new position by giving, in the delightful comedy *Spring in Park Lane*, the best, most amusing performance of his career.

Second Lady of Britain's Silver Screen—*you* say—is ever popular ANNA NEAGLE, who at 40 still looks incredibly girlish. Miss Neagle started out in life as a dancer; was at one time one of Mr. Cochran's famous Young Ladies. Is now married to producer-director Herbert Wilcox.

Lovely JANET BLAIR—so beautiful in this portrait she just *couldn't* be left out of our picture gallery—comes from the town of Altoona in Philadelphia. She's 26 years old, came to the movies by way of church hall entertainments and vocals with dance bands. Her real name is Martha Jane Lafferty—and at one time she had freckles!

"There but for the grace of God, goes God," someone once said of 32-year-old "wonder boy" ORSON WELLES, writer, director, producer and star of films. He could speak perfect English at 2; at 22 he was scaring America out of her wits by his radio production of the H. G. Wells story "War of the Worlds"; and at 25 he had written, directed, produced and starred in one of the most noteworthy films of all time, the tremendous *Citizen Kane*.

One of our best actors, seen far too seldom on the screen, is ROBERT NEWTON, son of an artist, who began his acting career by painting theatrical scenery. He also worked as a stage hand before he achieved his ambition and was given an acting part in one of the Birmingham Rep. productions. Born in Shaftesbury, in 1905, he was actually educated in Switzerland.

STEWART GRANGER has not always had the happiest choice of roles during his screen career, but he had one of the best parts for some time in this year's Technicolored *Cineguild* production BLANCHE FURY.

With a Spanish father, an Irish mother and a real name of Margarita Carmen Cansino, blonde—formerly red-headed—RITA HAYWORTH is as exotic as you might expect. She started as a dancer; indeed, with her father as partner, she danced her way round the world before starting in pictures in 1935 in *Dante's Inferno*. Was at her most alluring in *Blood and Sand*, twinkled most with Fred Astaire in *You'll Never Get Rich*. This year played opposite ex-husband Orson Welles in *Lady from Shanghai*.

32-year-old GREGORY PECK comes under the category once labelled by film critic Dilys Powell as the " Handsome Haggards ". He is somewhat unique in that he started his film career as a star and didn't have to work his way up. He was an expert sportsman until a spinal injury made him take life more quietly and he turned to acting. His Broadway success in " Morning Star " made him fair game for Hollywood. He comes from California.

Essentially British in looks and speech is PHYLLIS CALVERT, born in Chelsea in the year of the first Great Peace, 1918. She occupies a little niche all of her own; as a child studied as a ballet dancer and only switched to acting later. Is married to actor Peter Murray-Hill and has a 4-year-old daughter.

The passing years appear to take no toll of 1908-born, curley-haired FRED MAC-MURRAY, who takes tragic drama (*Double Indemnity*) and farcical comedy (*The Egg and I*) in his stride. To earn his college fees Mac-Murray sang and played with dance bands and it was with such an outfit he eventually found his way to Hollywood, where he worked his way up from extra to star in several hard lessons.

JANE WYMAN, star of many Warner films and this year co-starring with JAMES STEWART in *R.K.O. Radio*'s MAGIC TOWN. (Late 1948 or early 1949 release.)

FOUR MEN
and a GIRL

PATRICIA ROC (below) made 1948 her come-back year, for placed down to sixth place in the previous year's *Daily Mail* film poll, she climbed back into third place this time. And the gay musical she starred in recently, ONE NIGHT WITH YOU, has enhanced her chances for next year.

KIERON MOORE'S real name is Kieron O'Hannahan and he's as Irish as that makes him sound. He came to London to appear in the play "Desert Rats"; stayed to make a personal hit in O'Casey's "Red Roses for Me," on the strength of which he was given three starring roles before the public had even seen him on the screen!

DERMOT WALSH is another Dubliner who has made good in British films. He was apprenticed to a solicitor but eventually the stage won and he kicked-off his professional career in Dublin at 10/- a week. He came to England in 1945, to the Croydon Rep. First film was BEDELIA. 1948 productions include MARK OF CAIN, MY SISTER AND I and THEY CRACKED HER GLASS SLIPPER.

Since he came out of the Army and appeared at the Arts theatre, TREVOR HOWARD (left) has rocketed to stardom. One of his finest performances was in BRIEF ENCOUNTER; this year's appearances have included an impressive performance as the Fugitive in THEY MADE ME A FUGITIVE.

Australian JOHN McCALLUM (right), after repertory work in his own country, decided that his future lay in Hollywood. But dropping off here on the way, he was given a part in THE ROOT OF ALL EVIL. That brought him other offers. This year he has made a number of pictures, including MIRANDA and THE CALENDAR.

First result announced in 1948 was the annual Motion Picture Herald poll of so-called "Money-Making-Stars" of the year, published in January. These stars are voted for by British exhibitors who, after all, should surely know who are the film players that attract the customers. Here are the results:

BRITISH STARS who have appeared in films made in Britain : 1. James Mason : 2. Anna Neagle : 3. Margaret Lockwood : 4. John Mills : 5. Stewart Granger : 6. Patricia Roc : 7. Michael Wilding : 8. Deborah Kerr : 9. Robert Newton : 10. Trevor Howard.

INTERNATIONAL STARS who have appeared in any films : 1. Bing Crosby : 2. James Mason : 3. Anna Neagle : 4. Margaret Lockwood : 5. Bette Davis : 6. John Mills : 7. Alan Ladd : 8. Humphrey Bogart : 9. Ingrid Bergman : 10. Bob Hope.

WESTERN STARS : 1. Roy Rogers : 2. Gene Autrey : 3. William Boyd : 4. Randolph Scott : 5. Gary Cooper : 6. Ray Milland : 7. Johnny Mack Brown : 8. John Wayne : 9. Henry Fonda : 10. Fred MacMurray.

SHORT FILMS : 1. This Modern Age : 2. Walt Disney Cartoons : 3. March of Time : 4. Crime Does Not Pay : 5. Three Stooges Comedies : 6. Pathe Pictorial : 7. Guess What ? : 8. M.G.M. Technicolor Cartoons : 9. Fitzpatrick Travel Talks : 10. Speaking of Animals.

TOP MONEY-MAKING FILMS IN BRITAIN 1947 : 1. The Courtneys of Curzon Street : 2. The Jolson Story : 3. Great Expectations : 4. Blue Skies : 5. Duel in the Sun : 6. Holiday Camp : 7. Jassy : 8. Odd Man Out : 9. Frieda.

Next poll announced was that of the New York Film Critics, who chose Deborah Kerr as the best actress of the year, in *Black Narcissus* and *The Adventuress* (British title, *I See a Dark Stranger*). William Powell was chosen as the best actor for his performances in *Life With Father* and *The Senator was Indiscreet*. Best film : *Gentleman's Agreement*.

IN the *Daily Mail* poll, third of the annual National Film Awards, a record number of people voted ; 2,781,751 movie-goers taking the trouble to record their preferences. The result was that while Margaret Lockwood easily retained her position at the head of the list—and so scored a hat trick with 27% of the poll—John Mills (last year's runner-up) took over from James Mason as Britain's most popular film actor. Mason dropped to third place, which in view of his long absence is hardly surprising.

The list of most popular films reads strangely. Any conscientious critic will tell you that *Great Expectations, Odd Man Out* and *It Always Rains on Sunday* are all better films than *The Courtneys of Curzon Street*, yet they had to take 2nd, 3rd and 9th place respectively, under the latter ! Full results were :

	ACTORS :	ACTRESSES :	FILMS :
1	John Mills	Margaret Lockwood	The Courtneys of Curzon Street
2	Michael Wilding	Anna Neagle	Great Expectations
3	James Mason	Patricia Roc	Odd Man Out
4	Dennis Price	Jean Simmons	Jassy
5	Stewart Granger	Googie Withers	A Matter of Life and Death
6	David Niven	Joan Greenwood	Holiday Camp
7	Trevor Howard	Sally Gray	The White Unicorn
8	Jack Warner	Mai Zetterling	October Man
9	John McCallum	Valerie Hobson	It Always Rains on Sunday
10	David Farrar	Phyllis Calvert	Frieda

AT the annual "Oscar" festival in Hollywood in the Spring, the results of the Academy of Motion Picture Arts and Sciences included some awards which were generally anticipated and at least a few which were—at least to us over here—pretty astonishing. For instance, in the former category Ronald Colman's winning of top honours (Colman's first Oscar, though he has been in movies for more than 25 years) for best male screen acting performance of the twelve-months in *A Double Life* was more or less anticipated by anybody who had been following "form". But Loretta Young's walking off with the corresponding feminine honours with her performance in the amusing but never outstanding *The Farmer's Daughter* was something near incredible. Full results are too long to give here (and, in any case, I doubt if they are generally interesting to British moviegoers) but here are those that matter :

PRODUCTION :
"Gentleman's Agreement," Darryl F. Zanuck Production (20th Century-Fox).

PERFORMANCES :
Actor : Ronald Colman in "A Double Life." (Kanin Productions—U-I). Actress : Loretta Young in "The Farmer's Daughter." (R.K.O. Radio). Supporting Actor : Edmund Gwenn in "Miracle on 34th Street." (20th Century-Fox). Supporting Actress : Celeste Holm in "Gentleman's Agreement." (20th Century-Fox).

DIRECTION :
Elia Kazan in "Gentleman's Agreement." (20th Century-Fox).

WRITING :
Best written screenplay : "Miracle on 34th Street." George Seaton. (20th Century-Fox).

CINEMATOGRAPHY :
Black-and-White : Guy Green for "Great Expectations." (J. Arthur Rank—U-I). Colour : Jack Cardiff for "Black Narcissus." (J. Arthur Rank—U-I).

SHORT SUBJECTS :
Cartoons : "Tweetie Pie." Edward Selzer, producer. (Warner Bros.). One-Reel : "Goodbye Miss Turlock." Herbert Moulton, producer. (M.G.M.). Two-Reel : "Climbing The Matterhorn," Irving Allen, producer. (Monogram).

SPECIAL AWARDS :
"Shoe Shine." Italian production released by Lopert Films. Ken Murray for "Bill and Coo." (Republic). James Baskett for "Uncle Remus" in "Song of the South." (Walt Disney—R.K.O.). Special plaques to industry pioneers George K. Spoor, Thomas Armat, Albert E. Smith, and Col. William N. Selig. For scientific and technical achievements special plaques to C. C. Davis, Western Electric Co., Charles R. Dailey, Paramount Film Laboratories and Nathan Levenson, Warner Bros.

DOCUMENTARY PRODUCTION :
Short Subjects : "First Steps," United Nations Division of Films and Visual Information. Feature : "Design for Death," Sid Rogell, Executive producer : Thereon Warth and Richard O. Fleischers, Producers. (R.K.O. Radio).

In the American *Film Daily* poll (voting amongst 344 newspaper and magazine film critics, 120 radio commentators and local film exhibitors all through the U.S.) three British films were in the first ten, *Great Expectations, Brief Encounter* and *Odd Man Out*. Top of the poll was R.K.O. Radio's *Best Years of Our Lives*.

Odd notes about various polls in various spots about the world include : *Seventh Veil* voted best 1947 film by the Brazilian Critics' Circle ; Margaret Lockwood voted to head the list of favourite stars by cinema audiences in India and Czechoslovakia. In New York the National Board of Review) gave best actress as Celia Johnson (*Brief Encounter*) and best actor as Michael Redgrave (*Mourning Becomes Electra*, not yet seen here).

RISING ☆ STARS

and NEW FACES OF 1948

EACH year it is imperative, the business of films being what it is, that new faces appear upon the screen. Some of these newcomers, the lucky ones, because of sheer talent, strong personality, physical attractiveness or even through some peculiarity of manner, become sudden favourites and are rushed up to top stardom.

Others less fortunate, though not necessarily less talented, fail to make their mark and fall depressingly backwards either into the obscurity of minor, second features or possibly into an entirely different profession. (An insurance salesman and a lumberjack having made good film stars should mean, if you look at it logically, that a film star should be able to be a good insurance salesman or an excellent lumberjack !).

Anyway, though the star system may or may not be a good thing—certainly it is always under a certain amount of fire from one quarter or another—the fact remains that it would be a very brave or very uncommercially minded producer who would refuse to adhere to it.

This being so, and the loss of stars being a thing constant, the search for fresh star material is also constant. New faces, new talent, novelty ; that is the cry that echoes down the corridors of any film factory. In these circumstances it is all the more strange that so comparatively few new players should reach starring status in any one year.

1948 has produced its usual crop of possible new stars, both here and in America. But at this point it is difficult to forecast with anything like certainty those likely to go on up and those whose destiny lies not in the stars . . .

Time and public opinion will sit in judgement. So, it is not possible here to pretend to make any actual list of your future stars. All that can be done is take some of the players who have made their mark this year and of whom much will be expected in 1949. Some of the youngsters mentioned have already hit the bell and been made stars ; others have yet to prove that the promise they have so far shown is no mere flash in the pan. Yes, time will tell.

MICHAEL DENISON was an " unknown " when Associated British gave him star role of the young doctor. in *My Brother Jonathan*. His career started when visiting his wife, Dulcie Gray, to watch her make a test, he asked to play in it with her. The test proved successful—for both of them.

Left
Blonde, attractive BEATRICE CAMP-BELL, who emerged so triumphantly from the ordeal of her long and arduous part in her first starring film, *My Brother Jonathan*. She is Irish, her home being County Down, her father a Belfast Magistrate. She spent a year studying for a medical career before taking up the stage. She was spotted in Ireland and brought here by Frank Laun-der, who couldn't find a part for her. But A.B.P. did !

Unknown SHELLEY WINTERS gave a grand performance as the chatty little waitress with " connections " in the Ronald Colman film *A Double Life*. The critics all agreed newcomer Miss Winters has something, which means she will get more important roles during 1949.

JANE POWELL, *Metro-Goldwyn-Mayer's* lovely young singing star.

Left
Lovely South African actress EDANA ROMNEY made her first screen appearance in this country a few years back in *Alibi*. Then we saw nothing more of her until *Corridor of Mirrors* was shown in March, 1948. In this strange and quite lovely film Miss Romney not only co-starred with Eric Portman but also co-produced and co-scripted.

21-year-old JOSEPHINE STUART began her career as A.S.M. at the Watford Rep. There she was given her first opportunity to act, in Barrie's "Dear Brutus." Now she is one of the most promising of the Rank starlets. This year gave a most moving performance in *Oliver Twist*.

Below
Charlie Chaplin, who introduced to the screen in his films many girls who have since become stars (Paulette Goddard among them) proved he had lost none of his judgement in *Monsieur Verdoux*. MARILYN NASH showed beauty and considerable talent and should have a big Hollywood future.

Seen for the first time this year on British and American screens — though with 37 Italian made movies already to her credit — lovely Italian actress VALLI made a big enough hit to make a starry future certain.

Another young girl who has been given great opportunities during 1948 is 18-year-old blonde discovery SUSAN SHAW. Cast for an important role in the Launder and Gilliat film *London Belongs To Me*, she was subsequently kept very busy by Sydney Box.

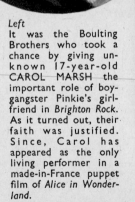

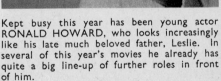

Left
It was the Boulting Brothers who took a chance by giving unknown 17-year-old CAROL MARSH the important role of boy-gangster Pinkie's girlfriend in *Brighton Rock*. As it turned out, their faith was justified. Since, Carol has appeared as the only living performer in a made-in-France puppet film of *Alice in Wonderland*.

Kept busy this year has been young actor RONALD HOWARD, who looks increasingly like his late much beloved father, Leslie. In several of this year's movies he already has quite a big line-up of further roles in front of him.

the social aspect of films and keep in touch with those Universities and other educational bodies in this country which have begun to take up motion picture studies.

In the branch of public relations the Academy will act as an organization representing the views of the creative film-makers in the United Kingdom. It is establishing contact with all groups concerned with the artistic and technical advancement of the film in the United Kingdom, the British Commonwealth of Nations and in all other countries. It has begun to co-operate with educational organizations for the better appreciation and understanding of the cinema, and will encourage the foundation of University departments of film studies. It will encourage, and possibly at a later date promote, research and experimental work. It will make awards of merit for outstanding artistic, technical and scientific achievements. Finally, the Academy is prepared to assist in the organization of film festivals at home and abroad.

PORTRAIT HEAD—FEMALE. (Two nominations).
Vivien Leigh in ANNA KARENINA. Photograph by Ted Reed.

its organizers sound men who know the Industry, and its potentialities are almost limitless.

One of the first public functions of the Academy was the exhibition of film stills, held at The National Book League Galleries from May 3rd to 25th. For this event a selection committee was formed consisting of :—Edward Woods (Chairman), Davis Boulton, Jack Dooley, Eric Gray, John Hardman, Ronald Neame, Wilfred Newton, John Myers, Wolfgang Suschitsky, and still photographers were invited to submit their best work so that from it could be selected a series of the most outstanding stills of the year. It was an excellent idea in every way and created a good deal of attention. The winning exhibits are illustrated on these pages.

Jean Simmons as Caroline in UNCLE SILAS. Photograph by George Cannons.

It has been suggested for many years that Britain should possess a Film Academy of this kind. As early as 24th April, 1929, George Pearson (now one of the first Honorary Members of the Academy) wrote in 'The Bioscope' urging the necessity for a similar organization. Now that nearly twenty years later the Academy has been founded, it is starting its activities at a period when the prestige of British film production stands higher than at any previous time in its history. The Academy's function is to help our film-makers to maintain and develop the standard of their work in every branch of the factual and the fiction film."

There's quite a lot more to the Academy even than all that, but I think that will suffice to show that its objects are good,

EXTERIOR. *SCOTT OF THE ANTARCTIC. Enlargement. Photograph by Dick Woodard.*

ACTION. *Anna Neagle as Judy in SPRING IN PARK LANE. Photograph by George Higgins.*

SCENE. *Laurence Olivier as Hamlet climbing in mist. Photograph by Wilfred Newton.*

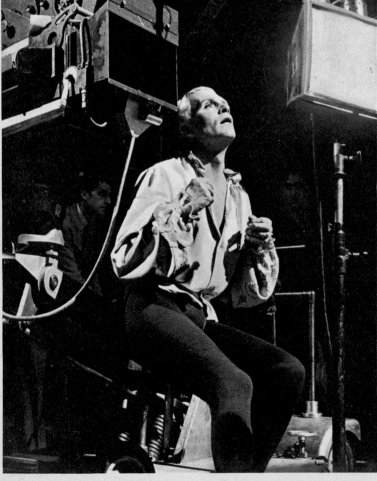

PRODUCTION. *Laurence Olivier with camera on HAMLET set. Photograph by Ian Jeayes.*

Kodachrome by Lippman

ROBERT YOUNG, MARGUERITE CHAPMAN and young friend in a typical scene from *Columbia's* RELENTLESS, a probable 1949 release.

H

A MATTER
of
MAKE-UP

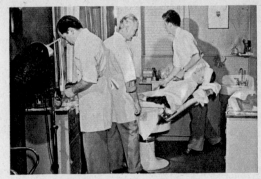

1 *Miss Moorehead arrives at the studios at 5 a.m.;
is soon settled comfortably in the make-up chair
while Buddy Westmore, the studio's chief make-up
artist, makes his preliminary preparations.*

2

*First her eyes
are painted
with a diluted
solution of
liquid adhesive
—are held in
position while
drying.*

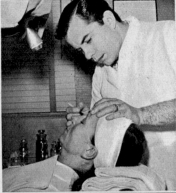

3

*The specially
made mask of
of imitation
wrinkled skin
is laid gently
on her face.*

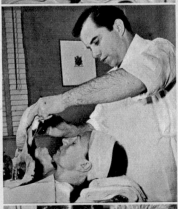

4

*It is kept in
position by
painting the tip
of the nose
and an area
just above the
eyebrows with
spirit gum.*

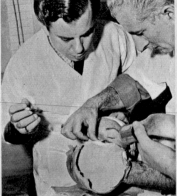

THE pictures on this and the next page give you a good idea of the art of the Make-Up Man. In *Universal-International's* THE LOST MOMENT, star AGNES MOOREHEAD had to look as though she's reached the age of 105. In the first picture (above) you see a portrait of Miss Moorehead as she really is, and in the last picture of the next page you see her as she appeared as the centurian on the screen. The transformation wasn't an easy one, as the following illustrations will show you.

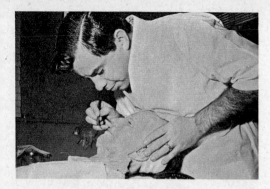

5 *The mask is then pressed on and carefully touched up here and there.*

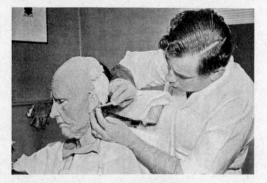

6 *It is fitted round the ears and neck, glued lightly to keep it in position.*

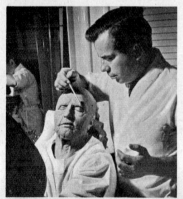

7 *Just before putting the wig on Buddy Westmore brushes Miss Moorehead's brows with a highlight grease.*

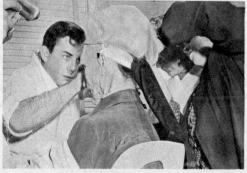

8 *Now comes the wig, which has to be fitted to the mask so that no join will show. A ticklish part of the job.*

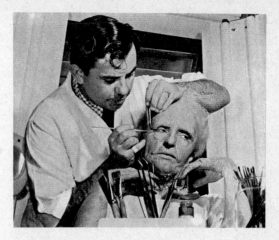

9 *All that remains now are the final touches, such as eyebrows and eyelashes.*

And so, at 8 a.m. three hours after she went into the make-up studio, Miss Moorehead was ready to go on the set and start her day's acting.

On this page, in complete contrast to the foregoing, you can see how entirely different an actor can be made to look without the addition of anything but a modicum of make-up. Above, HUMPHREY BOGART as he normally appears. Below, as he appears in the forthcoming *Warner* picture THE TREASURE OF SIERRA MADRE. All that Bogart did to effect the change was to let his hair and beard grow unkempt for a few days and to rub a little dirt into a sweating face. The total result of these very simple measures —as you can see for yourself—is to make a tough star appear a lot tougher.

Kodachrome by Scott

Jon Hall pulls his longbow and Michael Dunane prepares to take aim with his crossbow while lovely ladies Patricia Morrison and Adele Jergens look suitably tense and expectant. A scene from *Columbia's* 1949 release PRINCE OF THIEVES.

CHOOSING A FILM STORY

by
RONALD NEAME

Ronald Neame is a young man whose name is heard with increasing frequency in British Film Production. Recognised as one of the greatest lighting experts in this country, he has more recently turned his comprehensive knowledge of film-making to the field of production. He started as messenger at Elstree Studios in the silent picture era ; his father, Elwin, worked on many early British films. His mother is Ivy Close, who was one of England's loveliest film stars.

Ronald Neame has travelled almost all over the world making films. Successful movies his name has been associated with include *Major Barbara* and *One of Our Aircraft is Missing* (a picture for which he received an Academy Award nomination). He was director of lighting on Noel Coward's *In Which We Serve* and *This Happy Breed*. After this he joined Anthony Havelock-Allan and David Lean in the formation of a production company (*Cineguild*) with the idea of making unusual British films. The result has been a number of outstanding British movies, including *Blithe Spirit*, *Brief Encounter*, *The Passionate Friends*, *Great Expectations* (Ronald's first venture as a producer), *Take My Life*—and this year's finest British film—*Oliver Twist*.

WHAT am I going to make next ?
At the end of this year I am due to go on the floor with a new film. At the moment I've no more idea of what I'm going to make than you have. By the time this article goes into print I hope to have reached a decision, but for the next few weeks I shall spend many anxious hours looking for and finally deciding on what it is going to be.

A friend of mine said recently " I don't understand you film people. Here you are, surrounded with a wealth of wonderful material — stories of adventure, love stories, historical stories, detective stories, stories of the countryside, stories of the sea, plays by the greatest playwrights the world has produced, comedies, dramas, classics. You must be a lot of idiots if you can't find a film story somewhere."

Yes, it should be easy, shouldn't it ? But I assure you it isn't. Let's look a little closer at the problem. Let me explain, if I can, why it's so hard to decide what film to make.

In the first place I must tell you that a well-made, first-feature film capable of competing in the world market may cost anything from £200,000 to £400,000 according to its size, cast, and the length of time taken to shoot it. In order to have a chance of getting back the initial cost, it must appeal to the majority of film-goers in this country

and to a fair proportion in the rest of the world. To have a reasonable chance of succeeding my film must not be too experimental, it must, however, be unusual enough to allow for an original approach. It must not go over the head of the average film fan, but at the same time it must be advanced enough to interest the discriminating minority.

I would like my film to have heart, and warmth, and humour. I would like the audience to leave the theatre feeling that perhaps life isn't quite so bad after all. I would like my film to have excitement and suspense. I would like it to keep the audience in a continual state of wanting to know " what's going to happen next". I would like the characters to be well-drawn and true to life, but above all I would like my film to be a " movie ". It must have a story that can be told in a visual way. It must give the camera the opportunity of taking the audience by the nose and showing them things that can only be seen through the medium of the film.

I think the wealth of material my friend spoke about has already been considerably reduced!

I have recently been associated with two very successful pictures based on stories by Dickens, *Great Expectations* and *Oliver Twist*. I was tempted, therefore, to rely once again on a classic novel from yesterday, but many of the best of these are already registered by the American companies with the Motion Picture Association of America, and in any case there have been far too many period films in the last few years.

Perhaps before proceeding further I should explain what is meant by a picture being registered with the M.P.A.A.

If a writer has been dead more than 50 years his works enter the Public Domain and the film rights become free to the world. In the past film companies have sometimes commenced work on a script and sometimes even gone into production, only to find that another company had already started work on the same story. To prevent this the M.P.A.A., acting on behalf of nearly all the major producing companies in America, worked out a scheme whereby any of their members wishing to film a novel in the Public Domain could register the title. This having been done, all other members undertook not to make a film of that title without obtaining a release from the company concerned. About two years ago the British Film Producers Association entered into an arrangement with the M.P.A.A. and agreed to be a party to this scheme, thus a considerable number of British classics are not available to British film-makers. It took many weeks of discussion and argument before I was able to get a release from the American companies when we decided to film *Oliver Twist*.

The decision not to make a costume picture narrows down the choice of subject still further.

What material is there left? Contemporary novels, plays, short stories and, of course, original screen stories. Let's take the novels first. A great proportion of these are ruled out immediately because I would rather not make a war film. Perhaps in a year or two things will change . . . frequenters of the local Odeon may find the sound of a doodlebug interesting to listen to. At the moment we're still too close to the reality of war to find it entertaining.

Of the many novels written during the years just preceding the war there are few that aren't dated. We've changed a lot since those days—our whole outlook is different. The heros and heroines in the novels of the thirties seem rather irritating people to us who have lived through ten years of rationing and austerity, their values are quite different.

Among post-war novels there are many that would make fine films, but most of them are so depressing. Many of them start in a most promising manner. Three times last week I said at the end of the first fifty pages " Here's one at last ! " only to be let down with a bang on the last fifty pages because most of the characters, particularly the nice ones, finished up with nothing to live for.

If I am lucky enough to find the ideal book, I shall almost certainly find myself in competition with Hollywood. American film companies are wealthy and realising as they do that good stories are the life-blood of the industry, they are prepared to expend a great deal of that wealth in purchasing them. They think nothing of paying £50,000 for a novel or a play. They can afford it—we can't. Their market is much bigger than ours.

After thinking it over very carefully, I've come to the conclusion that the chances of my buying the novel I really want—if I find it—are about three to one against.

Most successful plays are also quickly snapped up by the Americans, even though, in my opinion, they don't make ideal film material. There are exceptions, of course—*This Happy Breed* and *Brief Encounter* for example—but for the most part they are static and, as is only natural, overloaded with dialogue. How many plays, I wonder, when adapted for the screen, have received from the critics the remark " This is nothing but a photographed stage play " ?

So much for plays. Now what have we left ? Short stories and original screen stories. Short stories sometimes make good films—Hemingway's *The Killers* for example — but more often than not the " stretching " spoils them. Original screen stories—I've kept these till last because, of course, they are the most important. What can be better for the screen than something written for the screen ? *The Best Years of Our Lives* is the classic example. In my opinion a perfect film.

There aren't many good screenwriters in this country—not more than ten, and that's being conservative. If any member of the Screenwriters Association reads this, will he take it for granted that he is one of the ten ?

Almost every writer thinks he can write a film. A few short weeks on a studio floor learning the difference between a long-shot and a close-up and he knows all about it. He couldn't be more wrong. To write a film script he's got first of all to learn all about film-making, he's got to spend months on production and if possible in the cutting rooms—but I'm drifting—let's get back to the choice of subject. Yes, I'd like my film to be made from an original if I'm lucky enough to find one, but even if I do there are still problems to be overcome before I reach a final decision, I've got to make sure I can cast it, and if possible cast at least one part with a well-known name. As I said before, I want my film to get its cost back ; a star name might add £20,000 to the budget, but by having that name I may take £80,000 more at the box-office.

We have very few star names in this country, as a result, many good stories, particularly those best suited to large-scale production, will have to go on the shelf.

That wealth of material has almost gone now.

No, it isn't easy to find an ideal film story. I'll find one in the end, of course, but for the next few weeks I shall continue to say something I seem to remember saying before—" What am I going to make next ? "

FIRST HALF YEAR
Films Released January to June

Randolph Scott (right) in THE ASSASSIN—Columbia.

Abie's Irish Rose. Sometimes amusing, occasionally somewhat embarrassing comedy based on the race rivalries of the Jews and the Irish ; in particular the feud of the fathers of a young Jewish lad and an Irish girl who get married. Cast : *Joanne Dru, Richard Norris, Michael Chekhov, J. M. Kerrigan, George E. Stone, Vera Gordon, Emory Parnell, Art Baker, Bruce Merritt, Eric Blore, Harry Hays Morgan.* Dir. and Pro. : *Edward A. Sutherland.* (Bing Crosby Productions—United Artists.) Rel. : Indefinite.

A Double Life. The story of an actor who became so immersed in the roles he played that he never knew which was the play and which was life ; became so involved with his playing of Othello that he unknowingly committed a murder and, to square things up, made the play's suicide the real thing. An intelligent story based on an intelligent, interesting theme and graced by a wonderful, Oscar-winning performance by *Ronald Colman*. Rest of cast : *Signe Hasso, Edmond O'Brien, Ray Collins, Millard Mitchell, Charles La Torre, John Drew Colt, Elizabeth Dunne, Art Smith, Sid Tomack, Harlan Briggs, Betsy Blair, Janet Warren, Marjory Woodworth, Shelley Winters, Philip Loeb, Joe Sawyer, Whit Bissell, Peter Thompson, Alan Edmiston, Wilton Graff, Claire Carleton.* In "Othello" : *Guy Bates Post, Frederick Worlock, Virginia Patton, Fay Kanin, David Bond, Thayer Roberts, Leslie Denison, Arthur Gould-Porter, Boyd Irwin, Percival Vivian.* In "A Gentleman's Gentleman" : *Elliott Reid, Georgia Caine, Mary Young, Percival Vivian.* Dir. : *George Cukor*. Pro. : *Michael Kanin*. (Universal-International). Rel. : June 28.

Against the Wind. Somewhat melodramatic and not always convincing story of the training in England of Belgian saboteurs during the war, their adventures when eventually they are dropped by parachute in their native land to carry on spying and sabotage. A confusing beginning leads to an exciting end, when the film really gets going, as the saboteurs rescue their key man from the Gestapo, flee, are chased, escape. Some excellent acting, especially from the French members of the cast (*Simone Signoret, Gisèle Préville, Paul Dupuis*) and several of the English (*Robert Beatty, Gordon Jackson, Jack Warner, Peter Illing, John Slater,* and screen newcomer *James Robertson Justice*.) Rest of cast : *Sybilla Binder, Hélène Hansen, Gilbert Davis, Andrew Blackett, Arthur Lawrence, Eugene Deckers, Leo de Pokorny, Rory Mac-Dermot, André Morell, Kenneth Villiers, Kenneth Hyde, Olaf Olsen, Philo Hauser, Martin Bradley, Sheila Carty, Margot Lassner, Guy Stephen Deghy, Jean Pierre Hambye, George Kersen, Duncan Lewis, René Poirier, Robert Wyndham.* Dir. : *Charles Crichton*. Pro. : *Michael Balcon*. (Ealing.) Rel. : Mar. 29.

Michael Chekhov, Joanne Dru and Richard Norris in ABIE'S IRISH ROSE—United Artists.

All the King's Men. Interesting, long documentary based on the training and duties of the various branches of the fighting services. With backgrounds of Sandhurst, the Tower, Windsor Castle and the Trooping of the Colour. Dir. : *Edward Eve*. (Angel-M.-G.-M.) Rel. : Feb. 16.

Ambushed. Cowboy *Russell Hayden*, foiling a gold-hungry band of bandits, foils them when they plan to ambush him by doing a little counter-ambushing on his own account. Rest of cast : *Bob Wills, Dub Taylor, Alma Carroll, Tristram Coffin, Donald Curtis, Jack Baxley, Leon McAulisse, Hailey Huggins*. Dir. : *William Berke*. Pro. : *Leon Barsha*. (Columbia.) Rel. : May 3.

An Ideal Husband. Extremely lavish, superbly Technicolored, highly polished Korda production of the famous Oscar Wilde play. Somewhat static, but witty and generally well acted. Beautifully dressed and photographed. Cast : *Paulette Goddard, Michael Wilding, Diana Wynyard, Hugh Williams, Sir Aubrey Smith, Glynis Johns, Constance Collier, Christine Norden, Harriette Johns, Michael Medwin, Michael Anthony, Peter Hobbes, Johns Clifford, Fred Groves, Michael Ward.* Dir. and Pro. : *Alexander Korda*. (London Films.) Rel. : Feb. 16.

Appointment With Fire. Clear, interesting documentary account of fire, both as a blessing and a curse. Well made, technically excellent and with a particularly good commentary by Alan Ivimey and Valentine Dyall. Cast of players includes : *John Kerr, Frank Hawkins*. Dir. : *Cecil H. Williamson*. (New Realm.) Rel. : March 22.

The Assassin. First-class Cinecolored Western from Zane Grey story about a cowboy (*Randolph Scott*) who, after killing his best friend decides to hang up his guns for good. He breaks his oath to revenge the murder of several of his friends by bad hombre *Bruce Cabot*. Rest of cast : *Barbara Britton, Dorothy Hart, Charles Grapewin, Steven Geray, Forrest Tucker, Charles Kemper, Grant Withers, John Miles, Griff Barnett.* Dir : *George Waggner*. Pro. : *Grant Withers*. (Columbia.). Rel. : June 21.

The Beast With Five Fingers. Typically incredible chiller-thriller about the hand of a famous pianist which takes on a horrid life of its own when its owner dies ; and goes crawling around putting in various odd spots of strangulation as an alternative exercise to playing Bach. Cast : *Robert Alda, Andrea King, Peter Lorre, Victor Francen, J. Carrol Naish, Charles Dingle, John Alvin, David Hoffman, Barbara Brown, Patricia White, William Edmunds, Belle Mitchell, Ray Walker, Pedro de Cordoba.* Dir. : *Robert Florey*. Pro. : *William Jacobs*. (Warner.) Rel. : June 28.

The Best Years of Our Lives. A very fine, perhaps a great film (certainly the best of its kind), about the men who come home (an army sergeant, an air-force captain and a sailor without hands) and the women, faithful and unfaithful, who wait for them. A familiar story by now on the screen, with a set of stock characters, the movie is lifted to the heights by its careful treatment, fine acting, warm understanding and dogged realism. Producer Samuel Goldwyn in his determination to keep his and everyone else's feet on the earth, even dispenses with make-up for his players, and as the crippled sailor introduces to the screen an actual handless veteran from the Pacific. As has been said with wit and truth elsewhere, a long (2¾ hours) film about a long story full of long thoughts. One of the best of the year. Cast : *Fredric March* (as the ex-sergeant banker), *Myrna Loy* (his whimsical wife)

Teresa Wright (daughter), *Dana Andrews* (soda-jerk air-hero), *Virginia Mayo* (unfaithful wife), *Harold Russell* (handless sailor) and *Cathy O'Donnell* (his sweetheart, a charming screen debut). Also : *Hoagy Carmichael, Gladys George, Roman Bohnen, Ray Collins, Minna Gombell, Walter Baldwin, Steve Cochran, Dorothy Adams, Don Beddoe, Victor Cutler, Marlene Aames, Charles Halton, Ray Teal, Howland Chamberlain, Dean White, Erskine Sanford, Michael Hall.* Screenplay by *Robert Sherwood*. Dir. : *William Wyler*. Pro. : *Samuel Goldwyn*. (R.K.O. Radio.) Rel. : April 5.

The Big Clock. Murder thriller with a neat twist. Editor *Ray Milland* is assigned the job of tracking down the murderer of his boss's girl-friend, soon finds all the evidence points to himself as the criminal. At the end he is trapped in his office building, trying desperately hard to evade capture while he makes a last-minute effort to smoke out the real murderer—his boss (*Charles Laughton*). Rest of cast : *Maureen O'Sullivan, George Macready, Rita Johnson, Elsa Lanchester, Harold Vermilyea, Dan Tobin, Lloyd Corrigan, Richard Webb, Henry Morgan, Tad van Brunt, Lucille Barkley, Elaine Riley, Robert Watson, James Burke, Frank Orth, Luis van Rooten.* Dir : *John Farrow*. Pro. : *Richard Maibaum*. (Paramount.) Rel. : April 19.

The Big Fix. Two ex-G.I.s go back to college, find love and a racket. Cast : *James Brown, Sheila Ryan, Noreen Nash, Regis Toomey, Tom Noonan, John Shelton, Charles McGraw, Charles Mitchell, John Morgan, Nana Bryant, Howard Negley.* Dir. : *James Flood*. Pro. : *Ben Stoloff*. (Pathe.) Rel. : June 28.

Blanche Fury. Ye olde time mellerdrammer type of story, adapted from the period thriller novel by Joseph Shearing ; about an illegitimate member of an old family who lives on as a servant with the idea of one day possessing the house of his ancestors, a house now owned by another family who have adopted the original owner's name of Fury. He gets the house in the end, by a double murder, but almost at once is tried and hanged for the crime. The film is better than the story, thanks to some of the best, most imaginative Technicolor yet seen on the screen and some excellent performances from *Valerie Hobson* (as Blanche, lovelier than ever before in a film), *Stewart Granger* (he's at his best too), etc. Rest of cast : *Walter*

Robert Mitchum and Jane Greer in BUILD MY GALLOWS HIGH—R.K.O. Radio.

Both JOHN WAYNE and LARAINE DAY both look rather worried in this scene from TYCOON, *R.K.O. Radio's* big Technicolored adventure of love in the Andes.

Ann Harding and Reginald Denny (right) in CHRISTMAS EVE—United Artists.

Fitzgerald, Michael Gough, Maurice Denham, Sybilla Binder, Edward Lexy, Allan Jeayes, Suzanne Gibbs, Ernest Jay, George Woodbridge, Brian Herbert, Arthur Wontner, Cherry London, Townsend Whitling, Amy Veness, Lionel Grose, Margaret Withers, Norman Pearce, Wilfred Caithness, James Dale, Cecil Ramage, Lance George, John Marquand, Vivien Dillon, David Ward, Sidney Benson, R. W. Haddow, M. E. Clifton-James, Derek Birch, Roddy Hughes, J. H. Roberts, Roy Arthur, Hilary Pritchard, Michael Brennan, Charles Saynor, Alexander Field. Dir.: *Marc Allegret.* Pro.: *Anthony Havelock-Allen.* (Cineguild.) Rel.: Mar. 22.

Blonde For a Day. When *Michael Shayne's* reporter pal gets shot up for trying to uncover a local racket, Shayne takes a hand in the business and solves another knotty problem. Cast: *Hugh Beaumont, Kathryn Adams, Cy Kendall, Marjorie Hoshelle, Richard Fraser, Paul Bryar, Mauritz Hugo, Charles Wilson, Sonia Sorel, Frank Ferguson, Claire Rochelle.* Dir.: Sam Newfield. Pro.: Sigmund Neufeld. (Pathe.) Rel.: Jan. 19.

Border Bandits. Nevada (*Johnny Mack Brown*) clears up a Western murder. Rest of cast: *Raymond Hatton, Riley Hill, Rosa del Rosario, John Merton, Tom Quinn, Frank La Rue, Steve Clark, Charles Stevens, Lucio Villegas, Bud Osborne, Pat R. McGee.* Dir.: Lambert Hillyer. (Pathe.) Rel.: Feb. 23.

Brighton Rock. Film based on the Graham Greene novel about the race gangs and underworld life of prewar Brighton ; more particularly about Pinkie Brown (*Richard Attenborough*), whose gang includes *William Hartnell, Wylie Watson* and *Nigel Stock*. Pinkie murders former gangster *Alan Wheatley*, then his own man, *Watson*, and finally tries to kill the sixteen-year-old girl (*Carol Marsh*) he has married to keep her quiet. A sordid story with various psychological and sociological undertones which are not brought out. But quite a brilliant film, technically ; cleverly directed, nicely photographed ; always exciting. Rest of cast: *Hermione Baddeley, Harcourt Williams, Charles Goldner, Virginia Winter, Reginald Purdell, Basil Cunard, Harry Ross, Campbell Copelin.* Dir.: John Boulting. Pro.: Roy Boulting. (Assoc. British.) Rel.: Jan 26.

Broken Journey. Conventional but quite well made story of an airplane that crash-lands in the Swiss Alps, the various reactions of the passengers and crew while they wait to be rescued. Based on a true incident when an American Army Dakota crashed in November 1946. Good general level of acting. Cast: *Phyllis Calvert, Margot Grahame, James Donald, Francis L. Sullivan, Raymond Huntley, David Tomlinson, Derek Bond, Guy Rolfe, Sonia Holm, Gray Blake, Andrew Crawford, Charles Victor, Gerard Heinz, Sybilla Binder, Amy Frank, Michael Allan, R. Stuart Lindsell, Mary Hinton, Jan van Loewen, Arthur Coulet, Leo Bieber.* Dir.: Kenneth Annakin. Pro.: Sydney Box. (Gainsborough.) Rel.: May 31.

Build My Gallows High. Called *Out of the Past* in America, based on the Geoffrey Homes novel which gives the film its British title, this is an extraordinarily complicated, often confusing story of a man who cannot escape his past. The man is *Robert Mitchum*, one-time private detective who, sent to catch up with and

bring back a gangster's (*Kirk Douglas*) girl friend, himself becomes romantically involved with her. They fly, but Mitchum's unpleasant partner, working for the gangster, tracks them down, whereupon the girl kills him. Mitchum goes to a small town to begin anew, falls in love with a local girl but is tracked down again, whereupon the girl kills the gangster and rides off with Mitchum into the arms of the police and death. The beautiful but homicidal girl is played by lovely *Jane Greer*. Rest of cast: *Rhonda Fleming, Richard Webb, Steve Brodie, Virginia Huston, Paul Valentine, Dickie Moore, Ken Niles.* Dir.: Jacques Tourneur. Pro.: Warren Duff. (R.K.O. Radio.) Rel.: Jan. 26.

C The Calendar. Straightforward adaptation of the Edgar Wallace racing story which has already done service as book, play and previous film. About some very unpleasant people and some very pleasant horses ; with an Ascot Gold Cup race final that is as thrilling as a horse race usually is upon the screen. *John McCallum* as the " broke " owner who toys with the idea of fixing a race (but doesn't), *Greta Gynt* as the girl who drops him when she finds he hasn't any money left, *Sonia Holm* as the good girl trainer who doesn't care about cash, *Raymond Lovell* as the gold-digger's final choice. And *Leslie Dwyer* steals the show with his delightful performance of the most impossible butler you'll ever meet, even on the screen. Rest of cast: *Charles Victor, Felix Aylmer, Sydney King, Noel Howlett, Barry Jones, Claude Bailey, Desmond Roberts, Diana Dors, Fred Payne, Cyril Chamberlain, O. B. Clarence.* Dir.: Arthur Crabtree. Pro.: Antony Darnborough. (Gainsborough). Rel.: June 28.

George Stephenson, James Kenny and Florence Stephenson in CIRCUS BOY— Gaumont British Instructional.

Chorus Girl. A minor British production about a girl who wanted to become a dancer ; winds up in the Palladium chorus. Cast: *Jacquelyn Dunbar, Alex Wright, Beth Ross, Beryl Trent, Maud Long, Rich Bellairs, Valerie Wainwright, Charmain Innes.* Dir. and Pro.: Randolph J. Tomson. (Renown.) Rel.: Feb. 16.

Christmas Eve. Confused and intricate story about a very rich old lady (*Ann Harding*), her crooked nephew (*Reginald Denny*) who is trying to get control of her fortune by having her certified as insane, and her three no-good adopted sons (*George Raft, George Brent, Randolph Scott*), who rush to her aid. Rest of cast: *Joan Blondell, Virginia Field, Dolores Moran, Douglass Dumbrille, Carl Harbord, Dennis Hoey, Clarence Kolb, Molly Lamont, John Litel, Walter Sande, Joe Sawyer, Konstantin Shayne, Andrew Tombes, Claire Whitney.* Dir.: Edwin L. Marin. Pro.: Benedict Bogeaus. (United Artists.) Rel.: Jan. 5.

Circus Boy. One of Rank's Children's Entertainment Films, made in first case with the label, " Not Intended for Adult Audiences," but so good that it was eventually decided to release it as an ordinary feature. About a boy who fails in the inter-school diving championship through loss of nerve, joins some circus friends during the holidays, regains it and then triumphantly takes the swimming cup for his school. Cast: *James Kenny, Florence Stephenson, George Stephenson.* Dir.: Cecil Musk. Pro.: F. A. Hoare. (G.B. Instructional.) Rel.: Feb. 2.

Corpse Came C.O.D. Frightened at being sent a trunk, with a body, glamorous film star

Adele Jergens decides to trust the press rather than the cops ; asks reporter *George Brent* to assist her. He unravels the crime, and others, and while doing it becomes "helped" by another reporter, *Joan Blondell*, with whom he falls in love. Rest of cast : *Jim Bannon, Leslie Brooks, John Berkes, Fred Sears, William Trenk, Grant Mitchell, Una O'Connor, Marvin Miller, William Forrest, Mary Fields, Cliff Clark, Wilton Graff.* Dir.: Henry Levin. Pro.: Samuel Bischoff. (Columbia). Rel.: June 18.

Corridor of Mirrors. Unusual, beautiful picture based on a fantastic story (by Chris Massie) about a beautiful young girl's strange fascination for a middle-aged artist with queer ideas. He has a wonderful and exquisitely furnished house, tries desperately to live in the past and spends his time dressing the girl in bygone fashions. When at last she breaks the spell it brings tragedy. Technically the film is most interesting, with new director Terence Young determinedly concentrating on sheer visual beauty and achieving a production of unusual grace and strange, macabre atmosphere. Introducing lovely new star *Edana Romney*, who plays opposite *Eric Portman* as the artist (a fine performance). Rest of cast : *Joan Maude, Barbara Mullen, Alan Wheatley, Bruce Belfrage, Leslie Weston, Hugh Sinclair, Thora Hird, Hugh Latimer, Lois Maxwell, Mavis Villiers, Christopher Lee, John Penrose, Valentine Dyall, Gordon Macleod, Noel Howlett.* Dir.: Terence Young. Pro.: Rudolph Cartier. (Apollo.) Rel.: April 12.

Counterblast. British-made story of germ warfare, with escaped Nazi *Mervyn Johns* masquerading as the professor he has murdered and being uncovered by young assistant *Robert Beatty*. Rest of cast ; *Nova Pilbeam, Margaretta Scott, Sybilla Binder, Marie Lohr, Karel Stepanek, Alan Wheatley, Gladys Henson, John Salew, Antony Eustrel, Archie Duncan, Karl Jaffe, Ronald Adam, Martin Miller, Aubrey Mallalieu, Kynaston Reeves, Jack Melford, Peter Madren, Frederick Schiller, Olive Sloane, Stevins Chambers, John England, Kenneth Keeling, Horace Kenney, H. G. Guinle.* Dir.: Paul L. Stein. Pro.: Louis H. Jackson. (British National-Pathe.) Rel.: June 14.

Crossfire. Extremely well-made, fast and exciting murder thriller—and one with a noteworthy difference. The murdered man is a Jew and the motive is racial prejudice. Though the thorny problem of anti-semitism is handled carefully it is handled, and that takes the movie out of the rut. *Robert Young* gives a finely realistic performance as the detective in charge, *Robert Ryan* is very good as the murderer. Rest of cast : *Robert Mitchum, Gloria Grahame, Paul Kelly, Sam Levene, Jacqueline White, Steve Brodie, George Cooper, Richard Benedict, Richard Powers, William Phipps, Lex Barker, Marlo Dwyer.* Dir.: Edward Dmytryk. Pro.: Adrian Scott. (R.K.O. Radio.) Rel.: Feb. 9.

Cry Wolf. Consistently gripping though not always completely convincing mystery thriller based on a novel by Marjorie Carleton. Its a story of inherited madness and grim suspicion, played against a background of a large and sombre house and its enormous grounds. *Barbara Stanwyck* plays the curious widow (she, rightly, doesn't believe her husband is dead) and *Errol Flynn* is opposite her as an enigma ; is he torturer and worse, or is he filled with good intentions ? The last few minutes of the movie provide the solution.

Bud Abbott, Iris Adrian and Lou Costello in WISTFUL WIDOW — Universal - International.

Rest of cast : *Geraldine Brooks, Richard Basehart, Jerome Cowan, John Ridgely, Patricia White, Rory Mallinson, Helene Thimig, Paul Stanton, Barry Bernard.* Dir. : *Peter Godfrey.* Pro. : *Henry Blanke.* (Warner.) Rel. : Mar. 15.

Dark Passage. Escaped convict *Humphrey Bogart* sets out to prove that he is no wife-murderer ; is helped by a girl (*Lauren Bacall*), with whom he falls in love. Tough, taut thriller which is technically brilliant and noteworthy for a set of outstanding cameo performances. Rest of cast : *Bruce Bennett, Agnes Moorehead, Tom D'Andrea, Clifton Young, Douglas Kennedy, Rory Mallinson, Houseley Stevenson.* Dir. : *Delmer Daves.* Pro. : *Jerry Wald.* (Warner.) Rel. : May 16.

Daughter of Darkness. Unrelentingly grim and sombre thriller, based on the Max Catto play " They Walk Alone " about a " strangely sexed " girl who murders the men that love her, a role played with tremendous effect by Irish newcomer *Siobhan McKenna.* Some lovely glimpses of Irish and Yorkshire scenery and, generally, an excellently contrived atmosphere of impending doom. Rest of cast : *Anne Crawford, Maxwell Reed, Grant Tyler, Honor Blackman, Barry Morse, George Thorpe, Denis Gordon, Liam Redmond, Arthur Hambling, George Merritt, David Greene, Nora O'Mahony, Ann Clery.* Dir. : *Lance Comfort.* Pro. : *Victor Hanbury.* (An Alliance Production—Paramount.) Rel. : Mar. 8.

Death in the Hand. Well-made minor British thriller based on a story by Sir Max Beerbohm ; about a man who forsees his own death and in his fear actually causes it. Cast : *Esme Percy, Ernest Jay, Cecile Chevreau, Carleton Hobbs, John Le Mesurier, Shelagh Fraser, J. Hubert Leslie, Nuna Davey, Norman Shelley, Wilfred Caithness, Thea Wells.* Dir. and Pro. : *A. Barr-Smith.* (Five Star.) Rel. : June 28.

Jorja Curtright, Robert Cummings and Marjorie Reynolds in HEAVEN ONLY KNOWS—United Artists.

The Devil On Wheels. A group of people are taught at great cost that not to drive safely brings death and misery. Cast : *Noreen Nash, Darryl Hickman, Jan Ford, James Cardwell, Damian O'Flynn, Lenita Lane, William Forrest, Sue England, Robert Arthur, Ann Burr.* Dir. : *Crane Wilbur.* Rel. : Mar. 8. (Pathe.)

Dick Barton—Special Agent. The famous radio serial character becomes involved in another typical thick-ear adventure, with Dick (*Don Stanard*), Snowey (*George Ford*) and Jock (*Jack Shaw*) defeating the machinations of the smugglers. Rest of cast : *Gillian Maude, Geoffrey Wincott, Arthur Bush, Alec Ross, Janice Lowthian, Morris Sweden, Farnham Baxter, Beatrice Kane, Ivor Danvers, Ernest Borrow, Colin Douglas.* Dir. : *Alfred Goulding.* Pro. : *Henry Halsted.* (Exclusive.) Rel. : May 9.

Drifting Along. Travelling Champ. Cowboy *Johnny Mack Brown* jumps in to aid *Lynne Carver* when her ranch is attacked by rustlers. Rest of cast : *Raymond Hatton, Douglas Fowley, Smith Ballew, Milburn Moranti, Thornton Edwards, Steve Clark, Marshall Reed, Jack Rockwell, Lynton Brent, Terry Frost, Leonard St. Leo, Ted Mapes.* Dir. : *Derwin M. Abrahams.* Pro. : *Scott R. Dunlap.* (Pathe.) Rel. : May 3.

Easy Money. Somewhat loosely constructed series of episodes centring around the Football Pools and what happens when various people win Big Money in them. There are four quite separate fictional stories, connected by a linking semi-documentary commentary about the inner workings of one of the big Pool firms. The first episode is a delightful family piece about the Staffords, with *Jack Warner* outstanding as the head of the house. Script and dialogue here are wonderfully casual and realistic. Second story concerns hen-pecked *Mervyn Johns* (also excellent) whose win leads to unhappiness and death. Third episode concerns a nighterie singer (*Greta Gynt*) and her seducing of Pools worker (*Dennis Price*) into trying to get a crooked win, and the last story is about a double-bass player who rebels against his instrument (*Edward Rigby* at his best). Highly amusing, thoroughly entertaining movie suiting nearly all tastes. Rest of cast : Episode One : *Marjorie Fielding, Yvonne Owen, Jack Watling, Petula Clark, Mabel Constanduros, David Tomlinson, Maurice Denham.* Episode II : *Joan Young, Gordon McLeod, David Horne, Grey Blake.* Episode III : *Bill Owen, Frederick Piper, Jack Raine, Dennis Harkin, John Blythe, Freddie Carpenter, Dancers from the London Casino.* Episode IV : *Guy Rolfe, Raymond Lovell, Frank Cellier.* Dir. : *Bernard Knowles.* Pro. : *A. Frank Bundy.* (Sidney Box—Gainsborough.) Rel. : Feb. 23.

Escape. Excellent new film based on the John Galsworthy play of the same title. Its about a man who kills a police detective during a brawl that follows an argument, resents the three-year sentence he gets as a consequence and breaks out of Dartmoor one typically foggy day. He escapes but he never gets free. During the gallant bid he makes he does find Romance, however, in the guise of helpful, daring young " county " horsewoman *Peggy Cummins.* Excellent performance by *Rex Harrison ;* another by *William Hartnell* as the very human detective who tracks him down. And a fine cameo of a clergyman by *Norman Woolland.* Rest of cast : *Jill Esmond, Frederick Piper, Marjorie Rhodes, Betty Ann Davies, Cyril Cusack, John Slater, Frank Pettingell, Michael Golden, Frederick Leister, Water Hudd, Maurice Denham, Jacqueline Clarke, Frank Tickle, Peter Croft, George Woodbridge, Stuart Lindsel, Ian Russell, Patrick Troughton, Cyril Smith.* Dir. : *Joseph L. Mankiewicz.* Pro. : *William Perlberg.* (20th Century-Fox British.) Rel. : May 16.

The First Gentleman. Somewhat slow and' stagey adaptation of the Norman Ginsbury play about the Prince Regent (later the heartily disliked George IV) and his battles with his headstrong and popular daughter Princess Charlotte. Amongst other things the First Gent. wants her to marry Prince William of Orange, while she determines to marry the handsome but penniless Prince Leopold (*Jean-Pierre Aumont*). Cecil Parker romps through the title role and newcomer *Joan Hopkins* is surprisingly good in her first film part as Charlotte. Rest of cast : *Ronald Squire, Athene Seyler, Margaretta Scott, Jack Livesey, Gerard Heinz, Joan Young, Anthony Hawtrey, Hugh Griffith, George Curzon, Betty Huntley-Wright, Tom Gill, Lydia Sherwood, Frances Waring, Amy Frank, Richard Shayne, Judy Beaumont, Olwen Brookes, Melissa Stribling, Drusilla Wills, Judith Nelmes, Dorothy Hammond.* Dir. : *Cavalcanti.* Pro. : *Jos. Freidman.* (Columbia-British.) Rel. : May 31.

Flight to Nowhere. A pilot becomes mixed up with a murder in Death Valley ; tracks down and traps the killer. Cast : *Alan Curtis, Evelyn Ankers, Jack Holt, Robert Armstrong, Micheline Cheirel, John Craven, Inez Cooper, Roland Varno.* Dir. : *William Rowland.* Pro. : *William B. David.* (Screen Guild.) Rel. : Feb. 23.

Fun and Fancy Free. In this Walt Disney takes a step backward towards his earlier, less experimental (Bambi) days with a two-par cartoon of feature length. First section concerns Bongo, a performing bear who, fed up with being star of the circus, runs away into the woods, where he meets surprises, romance (in the person of glamorous little she-bear Lulubelle) and danger—from villain Lumpjaw. A charming sequence, with Disney at his most delightful. Jiminy Cricket then goes on to the second episode in which Mickey plays Jack (with Goofy and Donald as his friends) and a wonderful new character, Willie the giant, is introduced, in a special Disney version of the old fairy story Jack the Giant Killer. Also

James Crabbe, Brian Weske and William Graham in JUST WILLIAM'S LUCK.—Alliance-United Artists (British).

introduced in this section are *Edgar Bergen* and his famous wooden personalities, Charlie McCarthy and Mortimer Snerd. (Walt Disney-R.K.O. Radio.) Rel. : Feb. 16.

Gentleman from Texas. Wells-Fargo agent *Johnny Mack Brown* cleans up Rimrock—with the aid of the lovely local editor ! Rest of cast : *Claudia Drake, Raymond Hatton, Reno Blair, Christine McIntyre, Tristram Coffin, Marshall Reed, Ted Adams, Frank LaRue, Steve Clark, Terry Frost, Tom Carter, Jack Rockwell, Lynton Brent, Pierce Lyden.* Dir. : *Lambert Hillyer.* Pro. : *Scott R. Dunlap.* (Pathe.) Rel. : Feb. 9.

Good Time Girl. Excellent film based on a true incident and a·topical problem. *Jean Kent* gives best performance of her career as a girl who leaves home because her father beats her, is double-crossed into taking the rap for a theft and gets three years in a reform school. The school isn't likely to reform anyone and *Jean* escapes. On the run she joins up with criminals, ends up with a prison sentence. First-class performances also from *Dennis Price, Griffith Jones, Flora Robson, Herbert Lom, Bonar Colleano, Hugh McDermott.* Rest of cast : *Peter Glenville, Nora Swinburne, Elwyn Brook-Jones, Jill Balcon, Beatrice Varley, Margaret Barton, Diana Dors, Garry Marsh, Harry Ross, Orlando Martins, Amy Veness, Jack Raine, Michael Hordon, George Carney, Zena Marshall, John Blythe, Joan Young, George Merrett, Phyllis Stanley, Betty Nelson, Renee Gadd, Danny Green.* Dir. : *David Macdonald.* Pro. : *Sydney Box.* (Sydney Box.) Rel. : June 14.

The Guilty. Don Castle kills Good Girl *Bonita Granville* thinking it is her faithless twin sister *Bonita Granville* ! Rest of cast : *Wally Cassell, Regis Toomey, John Litel, Ruth Robinson, Thomas Jackson, Oliver Blake, Caroline Andrews.* Dir. : *John Reinhardt.* Pro. : *Jack Wrather.* (Pathe.) Rel. : June 14.

Hard Boiled Mahoney. The original Dead End Kids start out to solve mystery of missing girl, become involved in a murder. Cast : *Leo Gorcey, Huntz Hall, Bobby Jordan, Gabriel Dell, Billy Benedict, David Gorcey, Bernard Gorcey, Patti Brill, Betty Compson, Pierre Watkin, Teala Loring.* Dir. : *William Beaudine.* Pro. : *Jan Grippo.* (Monogram-Pathe.) Rel. : Jan. 12.

Red Skelton and Virginia O'Brien in MERTON OF THE MOVIES—Metro-Goldwyn Mayer.

Heartaches. A murder mystery about a crooner who has to have someone to sing for him (*Kenneth Farrell*), his lovely press agent (*Sheila Ryan*) and her boy friend (*Edward Norris*). Rest of cast : *Chill Wills, James Seay, Frank Orth, Chili Williams, Charles Mitchell, Al La Rue, Phyllis Planchard, Ann Staunton.* (Pathe.) Rel. : Jan. 12.

Heart Royal. Romance on a Kentucky horse farm, with *Paul Campbell* winning over the hostile neighbours, putting right a legacy of fraud left by his father and marrying the lovely local horse doctor *Gloria Henry.* Rest of cast : *Harry Davenport, Mark Dennis, Clinton Rosemond, Harry Cheshire, Louis Mason, Oscar O'Shea, Ernest Anderson.* Dir. : *Robert Gordon.* Pro. : *William Bloom.* (Columbia.) Rel. : Mar. 8.

Heaven Only Knows. Somewhat strange Western, about a Heavenly Messenger (a relation of Mr. Jordan's ?) in the person of *Robert Cummings,* who comes down to earth to save the soul of bad-man killer *Brian Donlevy,* something achieved in the end by upward glances, churches and the killer falling in love with the local pastor's daughter. Strange is hardly the word, but it may serve. Rest of cast : *Jorja Curtright* (as the pastor's wife), *Marjorie Reynolds* (as the inevitable dance hall girl), *Bill Goodwin, John Litel, Stuart Erwin, Gerald Mohr, Edgar Kennedy, Lurene Tuttle, Peter Miles, Will Orlean.* Dir. : *Albert S. Rogell.* Pro. : *Seymour Nebenzal.* (United Artists.) Rel : Feb. 16.

Her Husband's Affairs. Amusing little comedy with husband *Franchot Tone,* involved with crazy inventor *Mikhail Rasumny,* steered out of trouble and disaster by smart wife *Lucille Ball.* Rest of cast : *E. E. Horton, Gene Lockhart, Nana Bryant, Jonathan Hale, Paul Stanton, Mabel Paige, Douglas Wood.* Dir. : *S. Sylvan Simon.* Pro. : *Raphael Hakim.* (Columbia). Rel. : June 18.

High Tide. Fast talking *Lee Tracy* in typical role as newspaper editor who covets the paper he is running to the extent of murdering his boss and anyone else who stands in his way. Talky, but fast and generally exciting. Rest of cast : *Don Castle, Douglas Walton, Julie Bishop, Anabel Shaw, Regis Toomey, Francis Ford, Anthony Warde, Argentina Brunetti, Wilson Wood.* Dir. : *John Reinhardt.* Pro. : *Jack Wrather.* (Pathe.) Rel. : Jan. 5.

I I Walk Alone. New style gangster movie with ex-convict *Burt Lancaster* out to get even with his double-crossing ex-partner, now wealthy nighterie owner *Kirk Douglas.* He meets *Douglas's* girl-friend *Lizabeth Scott* and falls in love with her. A smooth, sometimes exciting, occasionally dull movie with best performances coming from *Kirk Douglas* and *Wendell Corey.* Rest of cast : *Kristine Miller, George Rigaud, Mike Mazurki, Marc Lawrence, Mickey Knox, Freddie Steele, Dewey Robinson.* Dir. : *Byron Haskin.* Pro. : *Hal Wallis.* (Paramount.) Rel. : Jan. 19.

Idol of Paris. Somewhat incredible tale of good and evil, from the novel " Paiva, Queen of Love," by Alfred Schirokauer. About a ragman's daughter who escapes being raped by the skin of her teeth only to be turned out to starve in the cold, cold snow. In order to avenge her husband's death she pretends to be a bad lot, rivals the reigning Paris demi-monde and defeats her in a duel with whips. All very

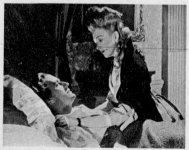

Peter Graves and Joyce Howard in MRS. FITZHERBERT—British National.

amusing if you look at it in the right way. Cast includes newcomer *Beryl Baxter.* Also : *Michael Rennie, Christine Norden, Miles Malleson, Andrew Osborn, Andrew Cruickshank, Keneth Kent, Margaretta Scott, Patti Morgan, Genine Graham, Henry Oscar, Sybilla Binder, Leslie Perrins, Campbell Cotts, John Penrose, Frederick Bradshaw, Donald Gray, April Stride, June Holden.* Dir. : *Leslie Arliss.* Pro. : R. J. Minney. (Premier.) Rel. : April 26.

Indian Summer. Rather lovely little movie about a judge (*Alexander Knox*) who, worried by work, money affairs and a wife who couldn't seem to care less about him, walks out on all his responsibilities to wander the countryside. He winds up in a wayside cafe ; falls in love with its owner, *Ann Sothern.* The film has charm and warmth and the nostalgia of old lavender. Beautifully acted by the two stars. Rest of cast : *George Tobias, Sharyn Moffett, Florence Bates, Frieda Inescort, Myrna Dell, Ian Wolfe, H. B. Warner, Martha Hyer, James Warren, Whitford Kane, Harry Hayden, Anita Bolster.* Dir. : Boris Ingster. Pro. : Michel Kraike. (R.K.O. Radio.) Rel. : Mar. 22.

It Always Rains on Sunday. One of the best British pictures of 1947. A simple story of the events that take place during a rainy Sunday in a small section of Bethnal Green ; the sheltering of an escaped convict, his further flight and eventual capture—and how it all affects Rose, once a barmaid, now a happily (!) married woman. What makes the film so brilliant is its superb realism of background, the almost diabolical insight into human character shown by director Robert Hamer and some wonderful acting ; especially by *Jack Warner* (detective), *John Slater* (Spiv), *Edward*

Ronald Howard, Maxwell Reed, Anne Crawford and Hector Ross in NIGHTBEAT —Harold Huth.

Chapman (family man), *Googie Withers* (Rose), *John McCallum* (the convict). Rest of cast : *Susan Shaw, Patricia Plunkett, David Lines, Sydney Tafler, Betty Ann Davies, Jane Hylton, Meier Tzelniker, Jimmy Hanley, John Carol, Alfie Bass, Frederick Piper, Michael Howard, Hermione Baddeley, Nigel Stock, John Salew, Gladys Henson, Edie Martin, Betty Baskcomb, Gilbert Davis, Al Millen, Vida Hope, Arthur Hambling, Grace Arnold, John Vere, Patrick Jones, Joe E. Carr, Fred Griffiths, Francis O'Rawe, David Knox.* Dir. : Robert Hamer. Pro. : Henry Cornelius. (Ealing.) Rel. : Jan. 1.

J Just William's Luck. First of a new series of British " family " films based on the famous character "William," star of so many Richmal Crompton stories. Unpretentious, simple but very wholesomely entertaining and quite amusing. Family consists of Mr. Brown (*Garry Marsh*), Mrs. Brown (*Jane Welsh*), Robert (*Hugh Cross*), Ethel (*Kathleen Stuart*) and, of course, William (*William Graham*). The three other boys in William's gang are Ginger (*Brian Roper*), Douglas (*James Crabbe*), Henry (*Brian Weske*). Rest of cast : *Leslie Bradley, A. E. Matthews, Muriel Aked, Audrey Manning, Hy Hazell, Ivan Hyde, Leslie Hazell, Peter Davis, John O'Horo, Michael Medwin, John Martel, Ivan Craig, Michael Balfour, John Powe, Joan Hickson, Patricia Cutts, Anna Marie, Jumble* (the dog). Dir. : Val Guest. Pro. : James Carter. (Alliance-United Artists.) Rel. : Mar. 22.

K King's Navy. Documentary about Naval training, showing how youngsters from establishments like Dartmouth and Deal are taught to be good tars and officers. Dir. : Edward Eve. (G.F.D.) Rel. : Mar. 22.

Noreen Nash, Robert Paige, Ted Donaldson and Jane Darwell in THE RED STALLION.

L Lady Chaser. *Inez Cooper* is wrongfully convicted of murder ; fiance *Robert Lowery* saves her by tracking down the real culprit, *Ann Savage.* Rest of cast : *Frank Ferguesn, William Haade, Ralph Dunn, Paul Bryar, Charlie Williams, Garry Owen, Marie Martino.* Dir. : Sam Newfield. Pro. : Sigmund Neufeld. (Pathe.) Rel. : Feb. 9.

The Lady from Shanghai. A strange, gripping murder mystery set against a constantly changing, by turns exotic and fantastic background. *Orson Welles* (who directs, produces and writes the screen play—from the Sherwood King novel) is cast as an Irish adventurer who meets a lovely lady (*Rita Hayworth*) and becomes involved with some strange, repellent characters and a plan for a particularly villainous crime. Superb performances by Welles, *Everett Sloane* (as a crippled, brilliant but entirely warped lawyer), *George Grisby* (as his crazy partner). Excellent and imaginative direction. A most interesting, unusual film ; and certainly a most intelligent one. Rest of cast : *Glenn Anders, Ted de Corsia, Erskine Sanford, Gus Schilling, Carl Frank, Louis Merrill, Evelyn Ellis, Harry Shannon, Wong Show Chong, Sam Nelson.* Dir. and Pro. : Orson Welles. (Columbia.) Rel. : April 19.

Lighthouse. Triangle troubles on a lighthouse. With waster *Don Castle* losing *June Lang* to steady *John Litel.* Rest of cast : *Marion Martin, Charles Wagenheim.* Dir. : Frank Wisbar. Pro. : Franklin Gilbert. (Pathe.) Rel. : Mar. 15.

M Mark of Cain. Highly melodramatic and not always credible adaptation of the Joseph Shearing period thriller " Airing in a Closed Carriage " ; the story of a man (*Eric Portman*) who hates his brother (*Patrick Holt*) and eventually murders him in order to steal his wife (*Sally Gray*). Rest of cast : *Dermot Walsh, Denis O'Dea, Edward Lexy, Therese Giehse, Maureen Delany, Helen Cherry, Vida Hope, Dora Sevening, Janet Kay, James Hayter, Helen Goss, Beryl Measor, Andrew Cruickshank, Marjorie Gresley, May MacDonald, Susan English, John Warren, Rose Howlett, Miles Malleson, William Mervyn, Noel Howlett, Arthur Howard, Hope Matthews, Olwen Brooks, Johnny Schofield, Sidney Bromley, Fred Johnson, Albert Ferber, John Hollingsworth, George Opoka, Jacqueline Robert, Tony Etienne, Willoughby Gray, Adrian Waller, James Carson, Mary Daniels, Jean Bowler, Wensley Pithy, Michael Logan, Nora Gordon, Christina Forbes, Colleen Nolan, Sheila Raynor.* Dir. : Brian Desmond Hurst. Pro. : W. P. Lipscomb. (Two Cities.) Rel. : Mar. 15.

Merton of the Movies. *Red Skelton* in picture of famous book, by Harry Leon Wilson, about the early days of the movies, a screen-struck cinema usher who gets his chance of film fame when he wins a big prize for heroism, dreams of playing Hamlet but is so hammy he is made a comedian instead ! Rest of cast : *Virginia O'Brien, Gloria Grahame, Leon Ames, Alan Mowbray, Charles D. Brown, Hugo Haas, Harry Hayden, Tom Trout, Douglas Fowley.* Dir. : Robert Alton. Pro. : Albert Lewis. (Metro-Goldwyn-Mayer.) Rel. : Mar. 22.

Mine Own Executioner. Adult, thoughtful, intelligent movie, teeming with bright ideas ; completely filmic in conception, writing and

The snow on her shoulders may be obviously synthetic but the beauty of face and figure are real enough :
a recent, wintery portrait of RITA HAYWORTH.

direction. Best British film for quite a while. The story of an honest and conscientious lay psychiatrist who, himself in something of a mental mess, accepts the responsibility of one of his patients murdering his wife and then killing himself. But the undertones of the tale are more important than the overtones, making the film one to see many times to appreciate fully. Technically the film is noteworthy, being full of imaginative little touches. Authoritatively directed and superbly acted by fine cast amongst whom *Burgess Meredith* as the psychiatrist and newcomer *Kieron Moore* as the patient, stand out. From the novel by *Nigel Balchin.* Rest of cast : *Dulcie Gray, Michael Shepley, Christine Norden, Barbara White, Walter Fitzgerald, Edgar Norfolk, John Laurie, Martin Miller, Clive Morton, Joss Ambler, Jack Raine, Lawrence Hanray, Helen Haye, John Stuart, Ronald Simpson, Gwynne Whitby, Malcolm Dalmayne.* Dir. and Pro. : Feb. 9.

Miranda. Most amusing, fairly broad comedy about a young doctor (*Griffith Jones*) who while on a fishing holiday in Cornwall gets an unexpected " bite " — Miranda, the lovely and man-loving mermaid (*Glynis Johns*). The fun starts when he brings her back to his Chelsea flat and introduces her to his wife (*Googie Withers*) as a patient who " can't walk." From the play by Peter Blackmore. Rest of cast : *John McCallum, Margaret Rutherford, David Tomlinson, Yvonne Owen, Sonia Holm, Lyn Evans, Maurice Denham, Howard Douglas, Anthony Drake, Philip Ray, Brian Oulton, Zena Marshall, Stringer Davis, Hal Osmond, Charles*

Franklin D. Roosevelt with wife and mother in THE ROOSEVELT STORY—Pathe.

Rolfe, Charles Paton, Charles Penrose, Frank Webster, Toni McMillan, Thelma Ray, Joan Ingram, Gerald Campion. Pro. : Betty Box. (Gainsborough.) Rel. : May 23.

Monsieur Verdoux. *Charles Chaplin's* first film in years and, most people will agree, a quite tremendous achievement. Chaplin as usual directs, produces, writes and himself stars in his picture, as well as composing the music for it. Forsaking his usual " Little Tramp " character, he plays a French bank clerk who, getting the sack because of the between-wars depression, starts out on a career of murdering lonely—and wealthy—old ladies ; doing it with grace, charm and immense good humour. A wonderful film, comic and serious by turns, sometimes immensely moving and often very nearly great ; full of irony, pathos, feeling, wit and—most essentially—intelligence. Apart from Chaplin cast includes : *Martha Raye, Mady Correll, Allison Rodman, Robert Lewis, Audrey Betz, Ada May, Isobel Elsom, Marjorie Bennett, Helen Heigh, Margaret Hoffman, Marilyn Nash, Irving Bacon, Edwin Mills, Virginia Brissac, Almira Sessions, Eula Morgan, Bernard J. Nedell, Charles Evans.* Dir. and Pro. : Charles Chaplin. (United Artists.) Rel. : Jan. 26.

Mrs. Fitzherbert. Unexciting, not always extremely well cast but quite sumptuously produced British Period (1780's) Piece ; the fictionalised story of the Prince Regent and Mrs. Fitzherbert, his morganatic marriage to, and final desertion of her. Cast : *Peter Graves, Joyce Howard, Leslie Banks, Margaretta Scott, Mary Clare, Frederick Valk, Ralph Truman, John Stuart, Helen Haye, Chili Bouchier, Julian Dallas, Frederick Leister, Eugene Deckers, Lawrence O'Madden, Barry Morse, Ivor*

Barnard, Lily Kann, Wanda Rotha. Dir. : Montgomery Tulley. Pro. : Louis H. Jackson. (British National-Pathe.) Rel. : Jan. 5.

Murder at Malibu Beach. When a couple of show girls are murdered and Charlie Chan is called in—the rest is inevitable ; false clues, artless humours, confusing actions, through all of which the imperturbable Chinese sleuth finds his way to the correct solution of the crime. Cast : *Sidney Toler, Mantan Moreland, Victor Sen Young, Tanis Chandler, Larry Blake, Kirk Alyn, Rita Quigley, Anne Nagel, Helen Gerald, Howard Negley, Lois Austin, Barbara Jean Wong, Minerva Urecal, Margaret Brayton, Bettie Best, Jan Bryant.* Dir. : Howard Bretherton. Pro. : James S. Burkett. (Pathe.) Rel. : Feb. 9.

My Brother Jonathan. A solid, satisfying, well acted and generally very well made adaptation of the Francis Brett Young novel about a young man who dreams of becoming a medical specialist but is side-tracked into becoming a general practitioner in a small Midland industrial town. New star *Michael Denison*, in the title role, gives a sympathetic and excellent performance in a long and arduous role ; newcomer *Beatrice Campbell* is impressive as the girl he loves, marries and loses. Cast also includes : *Dulcie Gray, Ronald Howard, Stephen Murray, Mary Clare, Finlay Currie, Arthur Young, J. Robertson Justice, James Hayter, Peter Murray, Jessica Spencer, R. Stuart Lindsell, Avice Landone, Wylie Watson, Hilda Bayley, Josephine Stuart, Fred Groves, Beatrice Varley, Felix Deebank, Eric Messiter, Paul Farrell, Jack Melford, David Ward, John Salew, Peter Hobbes, Kathleen Boutall, Wilfrid Hyde White, George Woodbridge, Leslie Watson, Merle Tottenham, Grace Denbeigh-Russell, Howard Douglas, Hilary Pritchard, Derek Farge, Eunice Gayson, Nora Gordon, Cameron Hall, Kathleen Heath, Paul Blake, Thora Hird, Maurice Jones, Vi Kaley, Fred Kitchen, Daniel King, Ruth Lodge, Johnnie Schofield, Jane Shirley, Wendy Thompson, Elsie Wagstaff, Hazel Adair, Grace Arnold, Ernest Borrow, Ernest Butcher, Raymond Cooney, Basil Cunard, Andrea Melandrinos, Beatrice Marsden, Elizabeth Maude, Janet Morrison, Sydney Monckton, Paul Sheridan, Desmond Newling, Alan Goodwin, Michael Caborne.* Dir. : Harold French. Pro. : Warwick Ward. (Associated British.) Rel. : Mar. 29.

N **News Hound.** Fourth and best of the new Bowery Boys series with *Leo Gorcey* uncovering a racket. Amusing comedy. Rest of cast : *Huntz Hall, Bobby Jordan, Gabriel Dell, Billy Benedict, David Gorcey, Christine McIntyre, Tim Ryan, Anthony Caruso, Bill Kennedy, Ralph Dunn, Nieta Bieber, John Hamilton, Terry Goodman, Robert Emmett Keane, Bernard Gorcey, Buddy Gorman, Russ Whiteman, Emmett Vogan Jr., John Elliott, Meyer Grace.* Dir. : William Beaudine. Pro. : Jan Grippo. (Pathe.) Rel. : May 16.

Nightbeat. British film about two ex-Commandos who join the police ; one to get on and gain promotion, the other to become involved with black marketeers and get the sack. Begins as quite interesting melo, dips into unintentional comedy. Cast includes a number of promising youngsters in Hector Ross, Maxwell Reed, Christine Norden, Ronald Howard. Others in the cast : *Anne Crawford, Fred Groves, Sidney James, Nicholas Stuart, Frederick Leister, Philip Stainton.* Dir. and Pro. : Harold Huth. (Harold Huth.) Rel. : April 12.

Night Comes Too Soon. A ghost story, from the Lord Lytton play " The Haunted and the Haunters," giving radio's famous spine-chiller *Valentine Dyall* (The Man in Black) his first film starring role. Rest of cast : *Anne Howard, Alec Faversham, Howard Douglas, Beatrice Marsden, Arthur Brander, Anthony Baird, Frank Dunlop, David Keir, Monti de Lyle, Nina Erber, John Desmond.* Dir. : Denis Kavanagh. Pro. : Harold Baim. (British Animated-Federated-Butcher.) Rel. : May 23.

O **One Night With You.** Gay, melodious and extremely charming British musical about a thistledown-light story about the romance of an Italian tenor (*Nino Martini*) and a lost English Miss (*Patricia Roc*) in Italy. Background of the Stresa lake Maggiore and the Isolla Bella island. Good fun, first-class light screen entertainment. Rest of cast :

Fred MacMurray, Ava Gardner and Roland Culver in SINGAPORE — Universal-International.

Bonar Colleano (superb as an excitable young Italian), *Hugh Wakefield* (as a truly-blue Britisher abroad), *Charles Goldner* (wonderful as an Italian film director) and *Stanley Holloway*, Willy Fueter, Irene Worth, Stuart Latham, Judith Furse, Brian Worth, Miles Malleson, Christopher Lee, Guy Middleton. Dir. : Terence Young (neatly and with imagination). Pro. : Josef Somlo. (Two Cities.) Rel. : June 7.

P **Personal Column.** *Lucille Ball* is employed by Scotland Yard as a bait to track down and catch a successful murderer of young women. A fairly ordinary whodunnit but with a sparkling cast and good production. Rest of cast : *George Sanders, Charles Coburn, Boris Karloff, Alan Mowbray, Sir Cedric Hardwicke, George Zucco, Joseph Calleia, Tanis Chandler.* Dir. : Douglas Sirk. Pro. : James Nasser. (United Artists.) Rel. : Mar. 8

Philo Vance's Gamble. Philo gets mixed up with a jewel gang and solves a triple murder. Cast : *Alan Curtis, Terry Austin, Frank Jenks, Tala Birell, Gavin Gordon, Cliff Clark, Toni Todd, James Burke, Francis Pierlot, Joseph Crehan, Garnett Marks, Grady Sutton, Charles Mitchell, Joanne Frank.* Dir. : Basil Wrangell. Pro. : Howard Welsch. (Pathe.) Rel. : May 31.

Possessed. *Joan Crawford* gives another most impressive performance as a woman whose unrequited love rules her life, drives her into a loveless marriage, to madness and murder. As the largely unwilling cause of it all, *Van Heflin* is excellent. Rest of cast : *Raymond Massey, Geraldine Brooks, Stanley Ridges, John Ridgeley, Moroni Olsen, Erskine Sanford, Gerald Perreau, Isabel Withers, Lisa Golm, Douglas Kennedy, Monte Blue, Don McGuire, Rory Mallinson, Clifton Young, Griff Barnett.* Dir. : Curtis Bernhardt. Pro. : Jerry Wald. (Warner.) Rel. : Jan. 12.

The Private Affairs of Bel Ami. Rather dreary screen adaptation of the Guy de Maupassant novel " Bel Ami," with *George Sanders* giving his usual, polished performance as the cad who comes to Paris and uses his fascination to women to bring him fame and fortune. Unfortunately it also in the end brings him death in the mud, when he over-reaches himself and, taking a nobleman's name as his own, is shot dead in a duel by the sole surviving member of the line. Rest of cast : *Angela Lansbury, Ann. Dvorak, Susan Douglas,*

Robert Newton, Dennis Price, Marcel Dalio and Guy Middleton in SNOWBOUND—Sydney Box—R.K.O. Radio.

Larry Parks, Ellen Drew, Ray Collins and Holmes Herbert in THE SWORDSMAN—Columbia.

John Carradine, Hugo Haas, Warren William, Frances Dee, Albert Basserman, Marie Wilson, Katherine Emery, Richard Fraser, John Good, David Bond. Dir.: *Albert Lewin.* Pro.: *David Loew.* (Metro-Goldwyn-Mayer.) Rel.: Jan. 19.

R **The Red Stallion.** Pleasant, familiar, Cine-colored story of a boy who finds an orphaned colt, brings it up and grows to love it. Boy, horse and dog become firm friends. Then grandma, owner of the ranch, goes broke and it looks as though she'll lose everything and the boy will lose the horse. Only a last minute win by the trio of friends brings a happy ending. Cast: *Ted Donaldson, Robert Paige, Noreen Nash, Jane Darwell, Ray Collins, Guy Kibbee, Willie Best, Robert Bice, Pierre Watkin, Bill Cartledge, Daisy, the dog.* Dir.: *Lesley Selander.* Pro.: *Ben Stoloff.* (Eagle-Lion.) Rel.: Mar. 15.

Riding the California Trail. Cisco Kid *Gilbert Roland* has another typical adventure, once more escapes the police and rides on . . . Rest of cast: *Martin Garralaga, Frank Yaconelli, Teala Loring, Inez Cooper, Ted Hecht, Marcelle Granville.* Dir.: *William Nigh.* Pro.: Scott R. Dunlap. (Pathe.) Rel.: Mar. 8.

Road to Rio. *Bob Hope, Bing Crosby* and *Dorothy Lamour* together again in one of their typically loosely-knit, gag-filled, very funny "Road" films. The two boys are dance band players who get mixed up with a lady mesmerist (*Gale Sondergaard*) and a strange gang. Rest of cast: *Frank Faylen, Joe Vitale, George Meeker, Frank Puglia, Nestor Paiva, Wiere Brothers, Andrews Sisters, Jerry Colonna.* Dir.: *Norman Z. McLeod.* Pro.: *Daniel Dare.* (Paramount.) Rel.: Mar. 29.

The Roosevelt Story. Carefully made documentary about the life and work of the great American president, compiled from newsreel cuttings and linked with a commentary. Pro.: Martine Levine and Oliver A. Unger in association with Harry Brandt. (Tola-Pathe.) Rel.: May 9.

S **Saigon.** *Alan Ladd* and *Veronica Lake* involved in adventures, squabbles and finally love in the Far East; he's a flier just demobbed and she's secretary to a Quisling. And screen newcomer *Luther Adler* walks off

Barbara White, Cyril Raymond and Sonia Dresdel in THIS WAS A WOMAN—20th Century-Fox.

with the acting honours. Rest of cast: *Douglas Dick, Wally Cassell, Morris Carnovsky, Luis Van Rooten, Mikhail Rasumny, Eugene Borden.* Dir.: Leslie Fenton. Pro.: P. J. Wolfson. (Paramount.) Rel.: Feb. 9.

Sarge Goes to College. Recuperating "Sarge" *Alan Hale Jr.*, of the U.S. Marines, gets involved with teen-agers at a college, saves the school show. Rest of cast: *Freddie Stewart, June Preisser, Frankie Darro, Noel Neill, Warren Mills, Russ Morgan, William Forest, Monte Collins, Margaret Braton, Frank Cady, Margaret Burt, Harry Tyler, Pat Goldin, Earl Bennett, Selmer Jackson, Arthur Walsh, Julie Mitchum, Joan Chapman, Don Ripps, Russ Morgan and His Orchestra, Jack McVea and His Band, Jam Session with Wingy Manone, Candy Candido, Joe Venuti, Abe Lyman, Les Paul, Jess Stacy, Jerry Wald.* Dir. and Pro.: Will Jason. (Pathe.) Rel.: June 14.

Scrapbook of 1922. Interesting documentary about life and the events of 25 years ago, with coverage of sport, politics, war, music and the people whose names were household words then. (Pathe.) Rel.: Jan. 26.

Singapore. After the war *Fred MacMurray* comes back to Singapore with the double purpose of unearthing his cache of smuggled pearls and to finding the girl he had been going to marry (*Ava Gardner*). He finds both, the first where he left them, the other as the wife of another man (Englishman *Roland Culver*). When he eventually goes he takes the girl, but not the pearls. Rest of cast: *Richard Haydn, Spring Byington, Thomas Gomez, Porter Hall, George Lloyd, Maylia, Holmes Herbert, Edith Evanson, Frederick Worlock, Lal Chand Mehra, H. T. Tsiang.* Dir.: John Brahm. Pro.: Jerry Bresler. (Universal-International.) Rel.: Jan. 5.

Snowbound. Incredible and strange-ending thriller (from the Hammond Innes novel " The Lonely Skier ") which starts out promisingly but fails towards the end and becomes merely wild. About a search for Nazi gold in a snow-bound hut high in the Alps, with British Intelligence officer *Robert Newton* on the one side and Nazi *Herbert Lom* and renegade British deserter *Guy Middleton* on the other. Somewhere caught in the middle are new continental star *Mila Parely*, *Marcel Dalio* and delightful *Stanley Holloway*. Rest of cast: *Willy Fueter, Richard Molinas, Catherina Ferraz, Massimo Coen, William Price, Gilbert Davis, Rossiter Shepherd, Zena Marshall, Lionel Grose.* Dir.: David MacDonald. Pro.: Aubrey Baring. (Sydney Box—R.K.O. Radio.) Rel.: May 2.

Son of Rusty. Second of the new Boy-and-Dog series, made mainly for the juveniles and with the sound moral that people shouldn't gossip. Cast: *Ted Donaldson, Stephen Dunne, Tom Powers, Ann Doran, Thurston Hall, Matt Willis, Rudy Robles, Teddy Infuhr, Mickey McGuire, Dwayne Hickman, David Ackles, Harlan Briggs, Griff Barnett.* Dir.: Lew Landers. Pro.: Wallace MacDonald. (Columbia.) Rel.: Jan 19.

Song For Tomorrow. Minor British melo-drama about a singer, the man who loves her and another man who loses her memory and loves her while he does. Cast: *Evelyn McCabe, Ralph Michael, Shaun Noble, James Hayter, Valentine Dunn, Yvonne Forster, Carleen Lord, Ethel Coleridge, Conrad Phillips, Martin Boddey, Sam Kydd, Lockwood West, Christopher Lee.* Dir.: Terence Fisher. Pro.: Ralph Nunn-May. (Highbury—J. Arthur Rank.) Rel.: June 28.

Speedway. Documentary interest picture about Speedway racing in general and the Wembley Lions team in particular. Showing training and racing, scenes both behind and in front of the stands. Dir.: Sam Lee. (Grand National.) Rel.: Feb. 2.

Stepchild. The drama of a broken marriage and its effect on the two children. A good theme somewhat marred by wordy and melo-dramatic treatment. Cast: *Brenda Joyce, Donald Woods, Terry Austin, Tommy Ivo, Gregory Marshall, James Millican, Griff Barnett, Selmer Jackson, Ruth Robinson.* Dir.: James Flood. Pro.: Leonard S. Picker. (Pathe.) Rel.: Jan. 5.

Roger Livesey and Kay Walsh in VICE VERSA—Two Cities.

Stork Bites Man. Pleasant, unpretentious, chuckly little comedy based on the topical problem of the difficulties of young married couples to get a house, and the scandal of landlords who won't let them have children ! Cast: *Jackie Cooper, Gene Roberts, Gus Schilling, Emory Parnell, Stanley Prager, Sarah Selby, Marjorie Beckett.* Dir.: Cyril Endfield. Pro.: Buddy Rogers, Ralph Cohn. (United Artists.) Rel.: Feb. 9.

Sweet Genevieve. A story of some extra-ordinary adventures in a most unusual kind of high school, where the scholars bet on horses, fiddle with new inventions and mix it with racketeers. Cast: *Jean Porter, Jimmy Lydon, Gloria Marlen, Ralph Hodges, Lucien Littlefield, Tom Batten, Kirk Allen.* Dir.: Arthur Dreifuss. Pro.: Sam Katzman. (Columbia.) Rel.: Feb. 2.

The Swordsman. Story of the bad old days of Scotland's history when the feuds amongst the clans were deep and bloody. Ace swordsman *Larry Parks* as the son of clan chief *Ray Collins*, falls in love with rival chieftain's (*Holmes Herbert*) daughter *Ellen Drew.* Completely incredible backgrounds, familiar story but all very enjoyable, thanks to the " Western " type of production. Cinecolored. Rest of cast: *George Macready, Edgar Buchanan, Marc Platt, Michael Duane, Robert Shayne, William Bevan, Nedrick Young, Lumsden Hare, Tom Stevenson, Harry Allen.* Dir.: Joseph H. Lewis. Pro.: Burt Kelly. (Columbia.) Rel.: Mar. 8.

T **This Was a Woman.** Somewhat stagey screen adaptation of the Joan Morgan play of the same title about a most unpleasant lady whose ambition and calculated sadism gradually outweigh her sense and lead her to the crime of murdering her husband. Remarkable study in malevolence by *Sonia Dresdel.* Rest of cast: *Walter Fitzgerald, Emrys Jones, Barbara White, Julian Dallas, Cyril Raymond, Marjorie Rhodes, Celia Lipton, Lesley Osmond, Kynaston Reeves, Noel Howlett, Joan Hickson, Clive Morton, Percy Walsh.* Dir.: Tim Whelan. Pro.: Marcel Hellman. (20th Century-Fox British.) Rel.: June 21.

Three on a Ticket. Michael Shayne, detective, looks into the little matter of a killed client ! Cast: *Hugh Beaumont, Cheryl Walker, Paul Bryar, Ralph Dunn, Louise Currie, Gavin Gordon, Charles Quigley, Douglas Fowley, Noel Cravat,*

Patricia Roc and William Owen in WHEN THE BOUGH BREAKS—Gainsborough.

Lovely, red-haired Irish girl MAUREEN O'HARA came back to England this year to star in *Twentieth Century-Fox's* new British film BRITANNIA MEWS (due for 1949 release). Her 1948 pictures included one of the best comedies of the year in SITTING PRETTY and another of her forthcoming pictures is *R.K.O. Radio's* THE LONG DENIAL—from which this study is taken.

Charles King, Sr., Brooks Benedict. Dir.: Sam Newfield. Pro.: Sigmund Neufeld. (Pathe.) Rel.: Mar. 22.

The Trespasser. Murder, rackets and night club singing in a more than somewhat complicated whodunnit. Cast: *Dale Evans, Warren Douglas, Janet Martin, Douglas Fowley, Adele Mara, Gregory Gay, Grant Withers, William Bakewell, Vince Barnett.* Dir.: Geo. Blair. Pro.: Wm. O. Sullivan. (Republic-British Lion.) Rel.: April 26.

Trigger Fingers. *Johnny Mack Brown* comes to the aid of his rancher friend when the gangsters try to get hold of his ranch by framing his son. Rest of cast: *Raymond Hatton, Jennifer Holt, Riley Hill, Steve Clark, Eddie Parker, Ted Adams, Pierce Lyden, Cactus Mack, Edward Cassidy.* Dir.: Lambert Hillyer. Pro.: Charles J. Bigelow. (Pathe.) Rel.: April 5.

U The Unfaithful. Domestic drama based on a topical problem; the lonely war-time wife who slipped just once, could not hurt her returned husband by telling him the truth, and was eventually found out. In this case the problem is highlighted by the fact that the old lover turns up again and is killed by the wife in her efforts to defend herself. Extremely capably acted by *Ann Sheridan* as the wife, *Zachary Scott* as the husband and *Lew Ayres* as the couple's friend and solicitor. Rest of cast: *Eve Arden, Jerome Cowan, Steven Geray, John Hoyt, Peggy Knudsen, Marta Mitrovich, Douglas Kennedy, Claire Meade, Frances Morris, Jane Harker.* Dir.: Vincent Sherman. Pro.: Jerry Wald. (Warner.) Rel.: Feb. 23.

Untamed Fury. About the feud of two boys which springs into life again when they meet in the swamplands after many years. Cast: *Gaylord Pendleton, Mikel Conrad, Leigh Whipper, Mary Conwell, Althea Murphy, Jack Rutherford, Charles Keane, Rodman Bruce, Paul Savage, E. G. Marshall, Norman MacKay.*

Dir. and Pro.: Ewing Scott. (Pathe.) Rel.: June 21.

V Vice Versa. Somewhat free adaptation to the screen by Peter Ustinov (who writes, directs and produces it) of the F. Anstey humorous story about a man who wishes he were a boy again—and finds his wish come true. He becomes a boy, his son, and his son becomes him! Of this Ustinov has made a satirical, pseudo-Victorian piece of purely parochial appeal. Cast is headed by *Roger Livesey* and *Kay Walsh* but acting honours are stolen by newcomer *James Robertson Justice*, with a terrific performance as the schoolmaster. Rest of cast: *David Hutcheson, Anthony Newley, Petula Clark, Patricia Raine, Joan Young, Vida Hope, Vi Kaley, Ernest Jay, Kynaston Reeves, Harcourt Williams, William ("Bill") Shine, Andrew Blackett, John Willoughby, Stanley Van Beers, Robert Eddison, James Hayter, Alfred (" Alfie ") Bass, Hugh Dempster, Peter Jones, James Kenney, Michael McKeag, Timothy (" Tim ") Bateson, Malcolm Summers, John Glyn-Jones, Frank Tickle.* Dir.: Peter Ustinov. Pro.: Ustinov and George P. Brown. (Two Cities.) Rel.: Mar. 1.

W When the Bough Breaks. Poor little *Pat Roc* learns that her husband is a bigamist just as her first child is born. A somewhat sad, sobby little story of mother love. Rest of cast: *Rosamund John, Bill Owen, Brenda Bruce, Patrick Holt, Cavan Malone, Leslie Dwyer, Sonia Holm, Torin Thatcher, Catherine Lacey, Edith Sharpe, Muriel George, Ada Reeve, Joan Haythorne, Edie Martin, Mary Stone, Sheila Huntington, Gerald Case, Jane Hylton, Noel Howlett.* Dir.: Lawrence Huntington. Pro.: Betty E. Box. (Sydney Box-Gainsborough.) Rel.: Feb. 2.

While I Live. Screen adaptation of the play "This Same Garden" by Robert Bell; somewhat too static, quite incredible. Interesting acting from *Tom Walls, Sonia Dresdel, Clifford Evans.* Story is about a repressed spinster, who drives her talented

young sister to suicide by her methods; then lavishes all her frozen love on a young girl when she mysteriously turns up in the house 25 years later. Rest of cast: *Carol Raye, Patricia Burke, John Warwick, Edward Lexy, Audrey Fildes, Charles Victor, Enid Hewit, Ernest Butcher, Johnny Schofield, John Martyn, Sally Rogers, Brenda Cameron, Diana Lake, Doreen Fischer.* Dir.: John Harlow. Pro.: Edward Dryhurst. (20th Century-Fox.) Rel.: Jan. 12.

Wild West. Singing cowboy *Eddie Dean* guards the Telegraph line against the attacks of Western racketeers and Indians. Rest of cast: *Roscoe Ates, Sarah Padden, Al Larue, Robt. "Buzzy" Henry, Louise Currie, Jean Carlin, Lee Bennett, Terry Frost, Warner Richmond, Chief Yowlachie, Bob Duncan, Frank Pharr, John Bridges, Al Ferguson, Bud Osborne.* Dir. and Pro.: Robert Emmett Tansey. (Pathe.) Rel.: May 24.

Woman on the Beach. Triangle troubles between a blind artist (*Charles Bickford*), a mentally unstable Coastguard Captain (*Robert Ryan*) and the artist's loose wife (*Joan Bennett*); with a background of the lonely, wind-whipped dunes on a desolate stretch of Atlantic coast. Rest of cast: *Nan Leslie, Walter Sande, Irene Ryan, Glenn Vernon, Frank Darien, Jay Norris.* Dir.: Jean Renoir. Pro.: (R.K.O. Radio.) Rel.: May 9.

The World is Rich. First-class Paul Rotha documentary; a strong, dramatic, intelligent and sometimes harrowing account of world food problems. The film makes a big point of the fact that while the earth is fruitful and there is potentially enough for all, and to spare, at the present time one in every three of the inhabitants of the earth is faced with hunger, if not actual starvation. This recital is allied to an appeal to plan intelligently and constructively through the United Nations Organisation. A most unusually well done and thoughtful picture. Dir.: Paul Rotha. (British Lion.) Rel.: Indefinite.

SECOND HALF-YEAR—Films Released July to December, 1948

A A Foreign Affair. Post-war comedy set in Berlin, where inquisitive congresswoman *Jean Arthur* shamelessly pursues U.S. Army Captain *John Lund*, who in turn industriously chases Nazi siren *Marlene Dietrich*. Rest of cast: *Millard Mitchell, Peter Von Zerneck, Stanley Prager, Bill Murphy, Raymond Bond, Boyd Davis, Robert Malcolm, Charles Meredith, Michael Raffetto, Damian O'Flynn, Frank Fenton, James Larmore, Harland Tucker, William Neff, George Carleton, Gordon Jones, Freddie Steele.* Dir.: Billy Wilder. Pro.: Charles Brackett. (Paramount.) Rel.: Nov. 29.

Alias A Gentleman. Typical *Wallace Beery* story about an ex-convict—with a heart of gold, of course—who decides to become a "gentleman." Rest of cast: *Tom Drake, Dorothy Patrick, Gladys George, John Qualen, Leon Ames.* Dir.: Harry Beaumont. Pro.: Nat Perrin. (M.G.M.) Rel.: Dec. 13.

Alice In Wonderland. Puppet film of the famous Lewis Carroll story with *Carol Marsh* playing Alice. There is a prologue and epilogue with real people. Made in France. No fuller details to hand at press-time. Rel.: Dec. 30.

All My Sons. Excellent screen adaptation of the Arthur Miller play which New York critics voted best of the year. About post-war tragedy of a wartime industrial profiteer (*Edward G. Robinson*) who shipped out defective aircraft parts, thus causing, indirectly, the death of his own pilot son. Rest of cast: *Burt Lancaster, Mady Christians, Howard Duff, Frank Conroy, Lloyd Gough, Arlene Francis, Henry Morgan, Elisabeth Fraser.* Dir.: Irving Reis. Pro.: Chester Erskine. (Universal-International.) Rel.: Oct. 11.

All Over the Town. Based on the R. F. Delderfield play about an ex-soldier who comes back to his job on his small-town newspaper with crusading ideas; how he is at first thwarted and then in the end triumphant. Cast: *Norman Wooland, Sarah Churchill, Cyril Cusack, James Hayter, Henry Edwards, John Salew, Fabia Drake, Ronald Adam,*

Patric Doonan, Edward Rigby, Sandra Dorne, Bryan Forbes, Eleanor Summerfield, Anthony Oliver, Eric Chitty, Patrick Macnee, Walter Horsburgh, Elise Bernard. Dir.: Derek Twist. Pro.: Michael Gordon. (Wessex.) Rel.: Late 1948 or early 1949.

Anna Karenina. Long, slow, lavish, obviously loving and occasionally dull screen adaptation of the famous Tolstoy story; reduced to its simplest terms, that of a women (married to a dull husband) who falls in love with an army officer and lets her passion drive her on from indiscretion to foolishness and suicide. *Vivien Leigh* plays Anna, *Kieron Moore* officer, and *Ralph Richardson* husband—the best performance. Rest of cast: *Hugh Dempster, Mary Kerridge, Marie Lohr, Frank Tickle, Sally Ann Howes, Niall Macginnis, Michael Gough, Martita Hunt, Heather Thatcher, Helen Haye, Mary Martlew, Ruby Miller, Austin Trevor, Ann South, Guy Verney, John Longden, Leslie Bradley, Beckett Bould, Judith Nelmes, Valentina Murch, Theresa Giehse, Michael Medwin, John Salew, Patrick Skipwith, Gino Cervi, Jeremy Spencer.* Dir.: Julien Duvivier. Pro.: Alexander Korda. (London Films.) Rel.: Sept. 27.

Another Shore. Whimsical comedy set in Ireland, from the story by Kenneth Reddin. About work-shy boy and interfering girl. Cast: *Robert Beatty, Moira Lister, Stanley Holloway, Michael Medwin, Sheila Manahan, Fred O'Donovan, Desmond Keane, Maureen Delaney, Dermot Kelly, Michael Golden, Michael O'Mahoney, W. A. Kelly, Wilfred Brambell, Michael Dolan, Madame Kirkwood Hackett.* Dir.: Charles Crichton. Pro.: Michael Balcon. (Ealing.) Rel.: Dec. 20.

Are You With It ? Musical with *Donald O'Connor, Olga San Juan, Martha Stewart, Lew Parker, Walter Catlett, Pat Dane, Ranson Sherman, Louis Da Pron, Noel Neill, Julie Gibson, George O'Hanlon, Eddie Parks, Raymond Largay, Jody Gilbert, Howard Negley, Charles Bedell.* Dir.: Jack Hively. Pro.: Robert Arthur. (Universal-International.) Rel.: Aug. 2.

Arthur Takes Over. What happens when the daughter of a small town family tells them that the sailor "friend" she introduced to them is really her husband. An amiable little domestic comedy. Cast: *Lois Collier, Jerome Cowan, Skip Homeier.* Dir.: Mal St. Clair. Pro.: Sol M. Wurtzel. (20th Century-Fox.) Rel.: July 12.

A Woman's Vengeance. Film based on the Aldous Huxley story "The Gioconda Smile," about an embittered spinster who murders a man's wife hoping to get him for herself and then, when her plans go wrong, tries to pin the crime on him. It comes out somewhat confusingly, though quite intelligently. Cast: *Charles Boyer, Ann Blyth, Jessica Tandy, Sir Cedric Hardwicke, Mildred Natwick, Cecil Humphreys, Hugh French, Rachel Kempson, Valerie Cardew.* Dir. and Pro.: Zoltan Korda. (Universal-International.) Rel.: July 5.

B Berlin Express. Topical, exciting post-war murder mystery filmed against a factual background of Paris and bomb-blasted Germany. Cast: *Robert Ryan, Merle Oberon, Charles*

Left to Right: Roman Toporow, Robert Coote, Paul Lukas, Merle Oberon, Robert Ryan, Peter von Zerneck and Charles Korvin in BERLIN EXPRESS—R.K.O. Radio.

Korvin, Paul Lukas, Robert Coote, Reinhold Schunzel, Fritz Kortner. Dir.: Jacques Tourneur. Pro.: Bert Granet. (R.K.O. Radio.) Rel.: Late 1948.

Best Man Wins. About a husband who came back and re-won his wife through his small son. Cast: *Edgar Buchanan, Anna Lee, Bob Shayne, Gary Gray, Hobart Cavanaugh.* Dir.: Ted Richmond. Pro.: John Sturges. (Columbia.) Rel.: Oct. 18.

Beyond Glory. Romantic drama concerning a war hero officer-cadet, his fight against a guilt-complex and his love for the widow of his Commanding Officer. Played against a background of the—to us—somewhat strange U.S. Military Academy. Cast: *Alan Ladd, Donna Reed, Harold Vermilyea, Conrad Janis, George Coulouris, Tom Neal, Richard "Dick" Hogan, Audie Murphy, George Macready, Henry Travers, Luis Van Rooten, Vincent Donahue, Margaret Field.* Dir.: John Farrow. Pro.: Robert Fellows. (Paramount.) Rel.: Indefinite. (Might be 1949.)

Big City. Sentimental little trifle about a small girl (*Margaret O'Brien*) adopted by Jewish *Danny Thomas,* Irish *George Murphy* and Protestant cleric *Robert Preston.* And how the three men quarrel and are brought together again by the love of the child. Rest of cast: *Betty Garrett* (Broadway singer making screen debut), *Lotte Lehmann* (famous soprano doing the same), *Karin Booth, Edward Arnold, Butch Jenkins.* Dir.: Norman Taurog. Pro.: Joe Pasternak. (Metro-Goldwyn-Mayer.) Rel.: Nov. 29.

The Big Punch. Conventional little story about crooked boxing. Cast: *Wayne Morris, Lois Maxwell, Gordon MacRae, Mary Stuart, Anthony Ward, Jimmy Ames, Marc Logan, Eddie Dunn, Charles Marsh.* Dir.: Sherry Shourds. Pro.: Saul Elkins. (Warner Bros.) Rel.: Aug. 23.

The Bishop's Wife. Polished, sophisticated comedy about a young bishop (*David Niven*) who prays for help and suddenly finds it has been given him in the person of a somewhat strange angel (*Cary Grant*). The bishop doesn't always appreciate the manner in which the angel works, especially when it comes to his concern over the bishop's lovely young wife (*Loretta Young*). All very amusing and, on occasions, quite moving. Rest of cast: *Monty Woolley, James Gleason, Gladys Cooper, Elsa Lanchester, Sara Haden, Karolyn Grimes, Tito Vuolo, Regis Toomey, Sara Edwards, Margaret McWade, Ann O'Neal, Ben Erway, Erville Alderson, Bobby Anderson, Teddy Infuhr, Eugene Borden, Almira Sessions, Claire Dubrey, Florence Auer, Margaret Wells, Kitty O'Neill, Isabel Jewell, David Leonard, Dorothy Vaughan, Edgar Dearing.* Dir.: Henry Koster. Pro.: Samuel Goldwyn. (R.K.O. Radio.) Rel.: Aug. 30.

Black Gold. The story of an Indian (*Anthony Quinn*), a Chinese boy he finds and adopts (*Ducky Louie*) and a horse which he loves and which brings him posthumous fame and fortune. In Cinecolor. Rest of cast: *Katherine DeMille, Elyse Knox, Kane Richmond, Moroni Olsen, Raymond Hatton, Thurston Hall, Jonathan Hale, Darryl Hickman, Charles Trowbridge.* Dir.: Phil Karlson. Pro.: Jeffrey Bernerd. (Pathe.) Rel.: July 5.

The Blind Goddess. The political machinations of a crooked peer (*Hugh Williams*) and the efforts of an honest young associate (*Michael Denison*) to expose him culminate in an exciting High Court trial. Written by a man who knows his courtrooms, Sir Patrick Hastings, K.C. Rest of cast: *Eric Portman, Anne Crawford, Nora Swinburne, Raymond Lovell, Claire Bloom, Frank Cellier, Clive Morton, Elspeth Gray, Maurice Denham, Cecil Bevan, John Stone, Philip Saville, Martin Benson, Cyril Chamberlain, Thora Hird, Rosemary Treston, Martin Miller, Marcel Poncin, Carl Jaffe, Geoffrey Denton, Noel Howlett.* Dir. and Pro.: Harold French. (Gainsborough.) Rel.: Oct. 18.

Blondie's Anniversary. Dagwood's affection for Blondie leads him again into those deep-waters he frequents so often. Cast: *Penny Singleton, Arthur Lake, Larry Simms, Marjorie Kent, Adele Jergens, Jerome Cowan, Grant Mitchell, William Frawley, Edmund MacDonald.*

Dir.: Abby Berlin. (Columbia.) Rel.: Nov. 15.

Body and Soul. Familiar but extremely well told story of a boxer who rises from the gutter to become world champ., who is tempted to throw a fight but in the end just can't, defies his mobster backer and goes in slugging to win the fight—and the girl, Lilli Palmer. Excellent performance by *John Garfield* as the boxer. Rest of cast: *Hazel Brooks, Anne Revere, William Conrad, Joseph Pevney, Canada Lee, Lloyd Goff, Art Smith, James Burke, Virginia Gregg, Peter Virgo, Joe Devlin, Shimin Rushkin, Mary Currier, Milton Kibbee, Tim Ryan, Artie Dorrell, Cy Ring, Glen Lee, John Indrisano, Dan Tobey.* Dir.: Robert Rossen. Pro.: Bob Roberts. (Enterprise-M.G.M.) Rel.: July 28.

Bond Street. Episodic story with a Bond Street background; one story is about a murderer (*Derek Farr*) who takes refuge with a no-good girl (*Jean Kent*), another is about a Sempstress (*Kathleen Harrison*) and a Lady (*Adrianne Allen*), another about a crippled girl-wife (*Patricia Plunkett*, excellent) and her twister husband (*Kenneth Griffith*, quite brilliant) while the very amusing linking story concerns *Roland Young's* efforts to get rid of a girl who suddenly turns up from Sweden (most attractive *Paula Valenska*) and looks like spoiling the marriage of his daughter. Interesting, often well acted but somewhat loosely constructed. Rest of cast: *Hazel Court, Ronald Howard, Robert Flemyng, Marian Spencer, James McKechnie, Joan Dowling, Leslie Dwyer, Charles Goldner, Mary Jerrold,* Dir.: Gordon Parry. Pro.: Anatole de Grunwald. (World Screenplays—Associated British.) Rel.: Aug. 2.

The Bride Goes Wild. Often crazy, generally quite amusing comedy—though not without dull patches—about a child-hating author of best-selling children's books and his uneven romance with the girl who wins a prize to illustrate his next opus. Cast: *Van Johnson, June Allyson, Butch Jenkins, Hume Cronyn, Una Merkel, Arlene Dahl, Richard Derr, Lloyd Corrigan, Elizabeth Risdon, Clara Blandick, Kathleen Howard.* Dir.: Norman Taurog. Pro.: William H. Wright. (Metro-Goldwyn-Mayer.) Rel.: July 12.

Bury Me Dead. A wealthy girl shocks everyone by returning home the day after her funeral. Murder thriller. Cast: *Cathy O'Donnell, June Lockhart, Hugh Beaumont, Mark Daniels, Greg McClure, Milton Parsons, Virginia Farmer, Sonia Darrin, Cliff Clark.* Dir.: Bernard Vorhaus. Pro.: Charles F. Riesner. (Pathe.) Rel.: Nov. 15.

Bush Pilot. Canadian-made picture about the Canadian Bush Pilots; with a little romance as well. Cast includes: *Jack La Rue, Rochelle Hudson, Austin Willis.* (Exclusive.) Rel.: July 5.

Caged Fury. Terrific paced Pine & Thomas circus melodrama with fights, fire, daring feats and altogether never a dull moment. Cast: *Richard Denning, Sheila Ryan, Mary Beth Hughes, Buster Crabbe.* Dir. and Pro.: William Pine, William Thomas. (Paramount-PT.) Rel.: Oct. 30.

Calling All Husbands. Henpecked husband *George Tobias* once again shows that a worm can turn to everyone's advantage. Rest of cast: *Lucille Fairbanks, Ernest Truex, George Reeves, Florence Bates, Charles Halton, Virginia Sale, John Alexander, Clem Bevans, Sam McDaniel, Elliott Sullivan.* Dir.: Noel Smith. (Warner.) Rel.: July 26.

Call Northside 777. Another of Fox's now-familiar but always excellent semi-documentary dramas made in the best "March of Time" manner. Reporter *James Stewart* finds out that 11 years previously a man has been unjustly convicted. Tense, factual, gripping. Rest of cast: *Richard Conte, Kasia Orazewski, Lee J. Cobb, Helen Walker, Betty Garde, Joanne de Bergh, John McIntire, Moroni Olsen, J. M. Kerrigan, George Tyne, Richard Bishop, Michael Chapin, E. G. Marshall, Walter Greaza.* Dir.: Henry Hathaway. Pro.: Otto Lang. (20th Century-Fox.) Rel.: Dec. 20.

Casbah. Third film of detective Ashelbe's novel which has seen previous screen service in France

as *Pepe Le Moko* and in America as *Algiers.* This time it has musical trimmings. *Tony Martin* now plays the thief, *Yvonne de Carlo* is the native girl who loves him and newcomer *Marta Toren* is the wealthy tourist who wins his heart and brings about his death. Rest of cast: *Peter Lorre, Hugo Haas, Thomas Gomez, Douglas Dick, Katherine Dunham, Herbert Rudley, Gene Walker, Curt Conway, Andre Pola, Barry Bernard, Virginia Gregg, Will Lee, Harris Brown, Houseley Stevenson, Robert Kendall.* Dir.: Bernard Hersbrun. Pro.: Nat G. Goldstone. (Universal-International.) Rel.: Late 1948.

Cheyenne. First-class if more or less routine Western; with plenty of riding-and-shooting action, simple humour and an uncomplicated story. *Dennis Morgan* as the gentleman gambler who sets out to trap stage-coach hold-up ace, The Poet. Of course he succeeds, in addition gets lovely *Jane Wyman*, the Poet's double-crossed, unloved wife. Rest of cast: *Janis Paige, Bruce Bennett, Alan Hale, Arthur Kennedy, John Ridgely, Barton MacLane, Tom Tyler, Bob Steele, John Compton, John Alvin, Monte Blue, Ann O'Neal, Tom Fadden, Britt Wood.* Dir.: Raoul Walsh. Pro.: Robert Buckner. (Warner.) Rel.: Aug. 9.

Daisy Kenyon. Romantic triangle drama with fashion designer *Joan Crawford* mixed up maritally with patient husband *Henry Fonda* and emotionally with unscrupulous lover *Dana Andrews.* Rest of cast: *Ruth Warrick, Martha Stewart, Peggy Ann Garner, Connie Marshall, Nicholas Joy, Art Baker, Robert Karnes, John Davidson, Victoria Horne, Charles Meredith, Roy Roberts, Griff Barnett, Tito Vuolo.* Dir. and Pro.: Otto Preminger. (20th Century-Fox.) Rel.: Late 1948.

Daybreak. Gloomy, sombre story about a hangman who lives on a barge, marries a waif without telling her his trade. A couple of suicides are thrown in as a horror make-weight. The film was so mutilated by the censor that producer Sydney Box felt constrained to complain that it was more or less ruined. Cast: *Eric Portman, Ann Todd, Maxwell Reed, Edward Rigby, Bill Owen, Jane Hylton, Eliot Makeham, Margaret Withers, John Turnbull, Maurice Denham, Milton Rosmer, Lyn Evans.* Dir.: Compton Bennett. Pro.: Sydney Box. (Sydney Box-G.F.D.) Rel.: July 5.

Deep Valley. Sombre, sad little story about Ma Saul (who once quarrelled with Pa and won't come downstairs at all now) and Pa (who resents this attitude more than a little) and their daughter Libby, who stutters on occasions and finds a strange romance with violent, escaped convict. The background is the Sauls' rotting house and the deep, mysterious Californian woods. The tragic ending is obvious always. Cast: *Ida Lupino, Dane Clark, Fay Bainter, Henry Hull, Wayne Morris, Willard Robertson.* Dir.: Jean Negulesco. Pro.: Henry Blanke. (Warner.) Rel.: July 19.

Desire Me. Tearful little triangle story about a girl (*Greer Garson*), her P-o-W husband (*Robert Mitchum*) and his ex-P-o-W friend (*Richard Hart*)—the cad who comes between them. The whole thing is played against a background of a fishing village along the Brittany coast. Rest of cast: *Morris Ankrum, George Zucco, Cecil Humphreys, David Hoffmann.* Pro.: Arthur Hornblow, Jr. (Metro-Goldwyn-Mayer.) Rel.: Dec. 6.

Dream Girl. Betty Hutton as the central character in a screen adaptation of the Elmer

James Stewart in CALL NORTHSIDE 777—20th Century-Fox.

Rice play about a girl whose day-dreams lead to dream lovers, and who is rescued from an emotional crisis by matter-of-fact newspaper man *Macdonald Carey*. Rest of cast: *Virginia Field, Patric Knowles, Peggy Wood, Walter Abel, John Abbott, Carolyn Butler.* Dir.: John Coonan. Pro.: P. J. Wolfson. (Paramount.) Rel.: Late 1948.

The Emperor Waltz. Quite outstanding Technicolored musical; lavish, spectacular, melodious (thanks largely to some lilting Strauss waltzes) and generally amusing. About the parallel romances of American talking-machine salesman *Bing Crosby* and Viennese Countess *Joan Fontaine*, and *Crosby's* mongrel terrier and *Miss Fontaine's* high-bred poodle bitch. The place is Austria and the time is 1901. Rest of cast: *Richard Haydn* (as the Emperor Franz Josef), *Roland Culver, Lucile Watson, Harold Vermilyea, Sig Ruman, Alma Macrorie, John Goldsworthy, Bert Prival, Roberta Jonay, Gerald Mohr, Harry Allen, Paul de Corday.* Dir.: Billy Wilder. Pro.: Charles Brackett. (Paramount.) Rel.: Late 1948.

Esther Waters. Victorian period piece about a serving girl who is seduced and weaned away from religion to the horses. A sad and sometimes sombre story. Cast: *Kathleen Ryan, Dirk Bogarde, Fay Compton, Ivor Barnard, Mary Clare, Julian D'Albie, Cyril Cusack, George Hayes, Morland Graham, Shelagh Fraser, Margaret Withers, Margaret Diamond, Lalage Lewis, Joseph Dillon, Philip Ashley, Harry Ross, Billy Rees, Fred Lane, Alex Parker, Nuna Davey, Barbara Shaw.* Dir.: Peter Proud. Pro.: Ian Dalrymple. (Wessex.) Rel.: Nov. 11.

The Exile. *Douglas Fairbanks, Jr.*, playing King Charles II, meets a lovely Dutch farm girl and goes to work on her farm as a handyman, keeping his identity secret meanwhile. All historians should see this interesting chapter of British history. . . . Rest of cast: *Maria Montez, Paule Croset, Henry Daniell, Nigel Bruce, Robert Coote, Otto Waldis, Eldon Gorst, Milton A. Owen, Colin Keith-Johnston, Ben H. Wright, Colin Kenny, Peter Shaw, Will Stanton, C. S. Ramsey-Hill, Gordon Clark, Lumsden Hare, Lester Matthews, Thomas P. Dillon, William Trenk, Fred Cavens, Alla Dunn, Torben Meyer, Grayce Hampton, Mary Forbes, Charles Stevens.* Dir.: Max Ophuls. Pro.: Douglas Fairbanks, Jr. (Universal-International.) Rel.: Nov. 1.

F

Fall Guy. Lost memory man gets mixed up in a murder. Cast: *Clifford Penn, Teala Loring, Robert Armstrong, Virginia Dale, Elisha Cook, Jr., Douglas Fowley, Charles Arnt, Jack Overman, Iris Adrian, John Harmon, Harry Strang, John Bleifer, Lou Lubin, Christian Rub, George Backus.* Dir.: Reginald Le Borg. Pro.: Walter Mirisch. (Pathe.) Rel.: Aug. 16.

Fallen Idol. Formerly titled **The Lost Illusion.** The story of a week-end in the life of an Ambassador's butler. During it he is suspected and cleared of the murder of his unpleasant wife and finds happiness with the girl he loves. Cast: *Ralph Richardson, Michele Morgan, Bobby Henrey, Sonia Dresdel, Denis O'Dea, Walter Fitzgerald, Jack Hawkins, Bernard Lee, Geoffrey Keen, Karel Stepanek, Danby Nichols, Joan Young, Hay Petrie, James Hayter, John Ruddock, Gerard Hinze.* Dir.: Carol Reed. Pro.: Alexander Korda. (London Films.) Rel.: Oct. 29.

The Fatal Night. Excellent British picture made on something like a record low budget of £17,000; an intelligent, well acted thriller from the Michael Arlen story "A Gentleman from America", about a practical joke which has tragic consequences. Cast: *Lester Ferguson, Jean Short, Leslie Armstrong, Brenda Hogan, Patrick Macnee, Aubrey Mallalieu.* Dir. and Pro.: Mario Zampi. (Anglofilm-Columbia.) Rel.: July 12.

The Flame. A crime story about nasty lot of people; *John Carroll*, playboy, plans with French nurse *Vera Ralston* for the girl to marry his half-brother *Robert Paige*—who has been given a very short time to live by the doctors—so that they can get the latter's fortune when he dies. Rest of cast: *Broderick Crawford, Henry Travers, Blanche Yurka, Constance Dowling, Hattie McDaniel, Victor Sen Yung, Harry V. Cheshire, John Miljan, Garry Owen, Eddie Dunn.* Dir. and Pro.: John H. Auer. (Republic-British Lion.) Rel.: July 12.

Forever Amber. Expensive, lavish, highly Technicolored screen adaptation of Kathleen Winsor's famous novel about Amber, the girl who just couldn't say No. She rises from the debtor's prison to the coveted position of Mistress to King Charles II. *George Sanders* as the King. *Linda Darnell* (Amber), *Cornel Wilde* (Bruce Carlton), *Richard Greene* (Lord Almsbury), *Glenn Langan* (Capt. Rex Morgan), *Richard Haydn, Jessica Tandy, Anne Revere, John Russell, Jane Ball, Robert Coote, Leo G. Carroll, Natalie Draper, Margaret Wycherly, Alma Kruger, Edmond Breon, Alan Napier.* Dir.: Otto Preminger. Pro.: William Perlberg. (20th Century-Fox.) Rel.: Sept. 27.

Fort Apache. First-class, long super-Western directed and produced by John Ford. Based on a true historical incident, finely played against the wonderful background of the Arizonian desert. *Henry Fonda* excellent as the embittered and mulish officer in charge of the outpost, *John Wayne* matching up to him as his sincere but disgusted aide. And some first-class supporting performances from *Shirley Temple* (as *Fonda's* daughter), newcomer *John Agar* (as the young officer she loves), *Ward Bond, Victor McLaglen, George O'Brien* and *Pedro Armendariz.* Rest of cast: *Irene Rich, Anna Lee, Dick Foran, Jack Pennick, Guy Kibbee, Grant Withers, Mae Marsh, Miguel Inclan.* Dir. and Pro.: John Ford. (Argosy-R.K.O. Radio.) Rel.: July 26.

The Foxes of Harrow. Lavish and lush screen adaptation of colourful, incident-packed best-seller by Frank Yerby. All about a handsome scoundrel (*Rex Harrison*), an illegitimate son who overcomes the social barriers of the period and the girl who hates—but marries him, of course. Background: New Orleans. Period: 1790-1840. Rest of cast: *Maureen O'Hara, Richard Haydn, Victor McLaglen, Vanessa Brown, Patricia Medina, Gene Lockhart, Charles Irwin, Hugo Haas, Dennis Hoey, Roy Roberts, Marcel Journet, Kenneth Washington, Helen Crozier, Libby Taylor, Renee Beard.* Dir.: John M. Stahl. Pro.: William A. Bacher. (20th Century-Fox.) Rel.: Dec. 27.

The Fugitive. The story of an Indian Catholic Priest in a Central American dictatorship who at last finds the courage of his convictions and dies bravely for his faith. Made in Mexico; slow, sombre, shot through with the hard Mexican sunlight and deep, black shadows, photographed with loving care and directed with complete mastery of his subject by John Ford, this is altogether a breathlessly beautiful film. *Henry Fonda* plays the inarticulate priest with all his usual sincerity, *Dolores del Rio* is the girl of easy virtue who is ever at his feet, *J. Carrol Naish* the traitor who betrays for gold and then regrets, and *Pedro Armendariz* represents the evil forces of the unsure dictatorship. Rest of cast: *Leo Carrillo, Ward Bond, Robert Armstrong, John Qualen, Fortunio Bonanova, Cris-pin Martin, Miguel Inclan, Fernando Fernandez.* Dir. and Pro.: John Ford. (R.K.O. Radio.) Rel.: Indefinite.

Fury at Furnace Creek. First-class Western with *Victor Mature* excellent as an itchy-fingered hero. Rest of cast: *Coleen Gray, Albert Dekker, Glenn Langan, Reginald Gardiner, Fred Clark, Charles Kemper, Roy Roberts, George Cleveland, Robert Warwick, Willard Robertson.* Dir.: Bruce Humberstone. Pro.: Fred Kohlmar. (20th Century-Fox.) Rel.: Late 1948.

G

The Gangster. Self explanatory title. *Barry Sullivan* is the man who wants money and doesn't care how he gets it. Belita is his girl. Rest of cast: *Joan Lorring, Akim Tamiroff, Henry Morgan, John Ireland, Sheldon Leonard, Fifi D'Orsay, Virginia Christine, Elisha Cook, Jr., Theodore Hecht, Leif Erickson, Charles McGraw, John Kellog, Eddie Maxwell, Dewey Robinson, Griff Barnett, Murray Alper, Shelly Winters, Larry Steers.* Dir.: Gordon Wiles. Pro.: Maurice & Frank King. (Pathe.) Rel.: Late 1948.

Gas House Kids Go West. The gang get mixed up with stolen cars. Cast: *Emory Parnell, Chili Williams, Vince Barnett, William Wright, Lela Bliss, Ronn Marvin, Ray Dolciame, Carl Switzer, Benny Bartlett, Rudy Wissler, Tommy Bond.* Dir.: William Beaudine. Pro.: Sam Baerwitz. (Pathe.) Rel.: Nov. 8.

Gentleman's Agreement. Rich, mature and brilliant screen version of the Laura Z. Hobson book on the theme of anti-semitism, with *Gregory Peck* giving a finely drawn, sincere performance of a man who, in order to write with authority of the subject of racial prejudice in America, for six weeks poses as a Jew and accepts all the humiliations, petty irritations and eventual heartbreaks the task brings him. Technically the film is spotless, acting throughout is of the very top class and altogether it well deserved the "Oscar" it won as the best motion picture of the year. Rest of cast: *Dorothy McGuire, John Garfield, Celeste Holm, Anne Revere, June Havoc, Albert Dekker, Jane Wyatt, Dean Stockwell, Nicholas Joy, Sam Jaffe, Harold Vermilyea, Ransom S. Sherman, Roy Roberts, Kathleen Lockhart, Curt Conway, John Newland, Robert Warwick, Louise Lorimer, Howard Negley, Victor Kilian, Frank Wilcox, Marlyn Monk, Wilton Graff, Morgan Farley.* Dir.: Elia Kazan. Pro.: Darryl F. Zanuck. (20th Century-Fox.) Rel.: July 26.

The Great Commandment. Story of the persecution of the Jews by the Romans and the teachings of Christ in and around Jerusalem about the time of his crucifixion; also the story of boy meets girl. Cast: *John Beal, Maurice Moscovich, Albert Dekker, Marjorie Cooley, Warren McCullum, Lloyd Corrigan, Ian Wolfe, Olaf Hytten, Anthony Marlowe, Lester Scharff, Albert Spehr, Marc Loebell, Harold Minjir, Earl Gunn, George Rosener, John Merton, Perry Evans, Stanley Price, D'Arcy Corrigan, Max Davidson.* Dir.: Irving Pichel. Pro.: John T. Coyle. (20th Century-Fox.) Rel.: Indefinite.

Green Dolphin Street. Long, sometimes spectacular, occasionally dreary film based on the novel by Elizabeth Goudge about two sisters (*Lana Turner*—tough—and *Donna Reed*—sweet) who fall in love with the same man, something of a weakling (new star *Richard Hart*). He really loves *Miss Reed* but through a completely incredible misunderstanding marries *Miss Turner*, who gradually makes a man of him. The situation is complicated by the fact that *Hart's* business partner, *Van Heflin*, is also in love with *Miss Turner*. The background is the Channel Islands and the New Zealand backwoods of 1840. The spectacle is provided by a terrific earthquake and a brush with the natives. Rest of cast: *Frank Morgan, Edmund Gwenn, Dame May Whitty, Reginald Owen, Gladys Cooper, Moyna Macgill, Linda Christian, Bernie Gozier, Pat Aherne, Al Kikume, Edith Leslie, Gigi Perreau.* Dir.: Victor Saville. Pro.: Carey Wilson. (Metro-Goldwyn-Mayer.) Rel.: Aug. 30.

The Guinea Pig. Screen adaptation of the Chetam Strode play of the same title. About the new Public School experiment, following the adventures of a scholarship boy who goes to a big school and has to find his feet there. Extremely interesting. Cast: *Richard Attenborough, Sheila Sim, Bernard Miles, Cecil Trouncer, Robert Flemyng, Peter Reynolds, Edith Sharpe, Anthony Nicholls, Joan Hickson, Herbert Lomas, Percy Walsh, Brenda Hogan, Hay Petrie, Olive Sloane, Wally Patch, Maureen Glynne, Anthony Wager, Robert Desmond, Basil Cunard, Norman Watson, Kynaston Reeves,* and *Jock McNaughton, Judy Manning, Lionel Stevens, Ambrose Day, Clive Baxter, John Forrest, Anthony Newley, Digby Wolfe, Oscar Quitack, James Kenney, Tim Bateson, Peter Howes, Richard Hart, Michael Braisford, Michael McKeag, Colin Stroud, Desmond Newling, George Bryden.* Dir.: Roy Boulting. Pro.: John Boulting. (Pathe.) Rel.: Oct. 18.

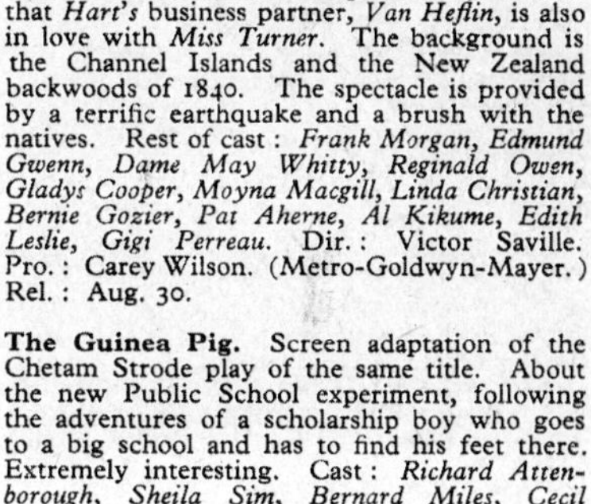

Van Helflin and Lana Turner in GREEN DOLPHIN STREET—Metro-Goldwin-Mayer

Percy Waram, Thurston Hall, Spring Byington, Ginger Rogers and Ron Randell in IT HAD TO BE YOU—Columbia.

H **Hamlet.** Brilliantly conceived, wonderfully executed screen adaptation to screen of Shakespeare's completely unfilmic play. The result is artistic, interesting and worthwhile, though—as one might expect in the circumstances—not completely successful. The acting is superb in every case, with *Laurence Olivier* himself giving one of the finest performances in the title role that this generation has seen. The background is the great castle of Elsinore, around and within whose walls the camera wanders unceasingly but never once gives the impression of anything but a photographed play. The Players: Royal Court of Denmark—*Eileen Herlie,* as the Queen, *Basil Sydney* as the King, *Laurence Olivier* as Hamlet, *Norman Wooland* as Horatio, *Felix Aylmer* as Polonius, *Terence Morgan* as Laertes, *Jean Simmons* as Ophelia. Servants of the Court: *Peter Cushing* as Osric, *Stanley Holloway* as Grave-digger, *Russell Thorndike* as Priest. Men at Arms: *John Laurie* as Francisco, *Esmond Knight* as Bernardo, *Anthony Quayle* as Marcellus, *Niall MacGinnis* as Sea Captain. The Play Within a Play: *Harcourt Williams* as First Player, *Patrick Troughton* as Player King, *Tony Tarver* as Player Queen. Dir. and Pro.: Laurence Olivier. (Two Cities.) Rel.: End of 1948 or beginning of 1949.

Hazard. *Paulette Goddard,* inveterate gambler, cured of her passion by pursuing detective *Macdonald Carey.* Comedy from the novel by Roy Chanslor. Rest of cast includes *Stanley Clements, Maxie Rosenbloom, Frank Faylen, James Millican, Percy Holton.* Dir.: George Marshall. Pro.: Mel Epstein. (Paramount.) Rel.: Not fixed at press-time—might be early 1949.

Here Come the Huggetts. Based on the success of the initial teaming of *Jack Warner* with *Kathleen Harrison* in "Holiday Camp," this is the first of a series of films about the Huggett family which are being built around them. A somewhat complicated story, full of typical cockney wit, wisdom and humour. Rest of cast: *Jane Hylton, Susan Shaw, Petula Clark, Jimmy Hanley, Diana Dors, Amy Veness, Peter Hammond.* Dir.: Ken Annakin. Pro.: Betty Box. (Gainsborough.) Rel: Dec. 6.

High Wall. Sombre, gloomy melodrama about a U.S. ex-army flyer (*Robert Taylor*) who one day comes back to find his wife in a somewhat compromising position. He "blacks out." When he comes to again and finds his wife dead, he thinks he has murdered her; the police get that idea too, and *Taylor* goes to an asylum to wait trial. While there pretty doctor *Audrey Totter* takes an interest in him and with the help of the miraculous "truth drug" finds *Taylor* innocent and uncovers the real criminal. Rest of cast: *Herbert Marshall, Dorothy Patrick, H. B. Warner, Warner Anderson, Moroni Olsen.* Dir.: Curtis Bernhardt. Pro.: Robert Lord. (Metro-Goldwyn-Mayer.) Rel.: Aug. 16.

Homecoming. Sentimental but extremely well acted triangle drama about a doctor (*Clark Gable*) who falls in love with the nurse (*Lana Turner*) who has accompanied him through all his wartime adventures—but when she is killed, he returns to his understanding, waiting wife (*Anne Baxter*) Excellently and steadily entertaining. Rest of cast: *John Hodiak, Gladys Cooper, Ray Collins, Marshall Thompson,*

Cameron Mitchell. Dir.: Mervyn LeRoy. Pro.: Sidney Franklin and Gottfried Reinhardt. (Metro-Goldwyn-Mayer.) Rel.: Nov. 8.

I **If Winter Comes.** M.-G.-M.'s remake of the old weepie (based on the novel by A. S. M. Hutchinson) comes out surprisingly well in its new coat, largely because of some sincere performances from *Walter Pidgeon* (as Mark, the gentle, firm and long suffering hero), *Deborah Kerr* (as the girl who loves him but marries another for some obscure reason) and *Janet Leigh* (Effie, who gets into trouble and, when named as co-respondent in a divorce brought by Mark's wife—*Angela Lansbury*—takes her own life). Rest of cast: *Binnie Barnes, Dame May Whitty, Rene Ray, Virginia Keiley, Reginald Owen, John Abbott, Rhys Williams, Hugh French, Dennis Hoey, Nicholas Joy, Halliwell Hobbes, Victor Wood, Hugh Green, James Wethered, Owen McGiveney.* Dir.: Victor Saville. Pro.: Padro S. Berman. (Metro-Goldwyn-Mayer.) Rel.: Sept. 20.

If You Knew Susie. Banjo-eyed *Eddie Cantor* returns to the screen after a considerable absence, teamed with comedienne *Joan Davis* in a comedy-musical about two vaudeville performers which introduces every familiar Cantor ingredient down to the bevies of beautiful girls. Rest of cast: *Allyn Joslyn, Sheldon Leonard, Charles Dingle, Phil Brown, Joe Sawyer, Douglas Fowley, Margaret Kerry, Bobby Driscoll, Dick Humphreys, Howard Freeman, Mabel Paige, Sig Ruman, Fritz Feld, Isabel Randolph.* Dir.: Gordon M. Douglas. Pro.: Jack J. Gross. (R.K.O. Radio.) Rel.: Sept. 20.

I Love Trouble. Average little detective tale with private "eye" *Franchot Tone* trying to solve the death of one lovely lady, becoming involved with no less than five others. In the end he accuses his client of murder—which isn't good for business—but makes up for that by marrying *Janet Blair.* Rest of cast: *Janis Carter, Adele Jergens, Glenda Farrell, Steven Geray, Tom Powers, Lynn Merrick, John Ireland.* Dir. and Pro.: S. Sylvan Simon. (Columbia.) Rel.: Aug. 9.

I Remember Mama. Warm, charming movie based on the book "Mama's Bank Account" and consisting of a series of loosely connected but always amusing incidents in the life of Mama (*Irene Dunne*), as remembered by daughter (*Barbara Bel Geddes*). For this performance *Miss Dunne* has been deservedly tipped as next year's Oscar winner. Well named "One of the happiest films of 1948." Rest of cast: *Oscar Homolka, Philip Dorn, Cedric Hardwicke, Edgar Bergen, Rudy Vallee, Barbara O'Neil, Florence Bates, Peggy McIntyre, June Hedin, Steve Brown, Ellen Corby, Hope Landin, Edith Evanson, Tommy Ivo.* Dir. and Pro.: George Stevens. (R.K.O. Radio.) Rel.: Aug. 23.

The Iron Curtain. Factual story of the uncovering of a Russian spy ring in Canada, based on the disclosures of the Royal Commission set up to investigate Soviet Underground activities. Made in factual, dynamic "March of Time" manner, with *Dana Andrews* as the Russian cipher clerk who gives the show away, *Gene Tierney* as his wife. Rest of cast: *June Havoc, Berry Kroeger, Edna Best, Stefan Schnabel, Nicholas Joy, Eduard Franz, Frederic Tozere, Noel Cravat, Christopher Robin Olsen, Peter Whitney, Leslie Barrie, Mauritz Hugo, John Shay, Victor Wood, Anne Curson, Helena Dare, Eula Morgan, Reed Hadley, John Ridgeley.* Dir.: William A. Wellman. Pro.: Sol C. Siegel. (20th Century-Fox.) Rel.: Sept. 6.

It Had To Be You. Completely crazy comedy with a story that defies outlining. Roughly it's about an heiress who, three times brought to the altar, can't say Yes at the critical moment. Then she meets fireman *Cornel Wilde*—and finds the word easy. None of it makes sense and not enough of it makes fun, though as the girl delightful *Ginger Rogers* tries very hard to make it do so. Rest of cast: *Percy Waram, Spring Byington, Ron Randell, Thurston Hall, Charles Evans, William Bevan.* Dir.: Don Hartman and Rudolph Mate. Pro.: Don Hartman. (Columbia.) Rel.: Sept. 9.

J **Jinx Money.** Better than average Bowery Boys comedy; they find fifty thousand dollars and at once become involved in a series of

murders. Cast: *Leo Gorcey, Huntz Hall, Billy Benedict, David Gorcey, Benny Bartlett, Gabriel Dell, Betty Caldwell, Sheldon Leonard, Donald MacBride, Wanda McKay, Lucien Littlefield, Bernard Gorcey, Benny Baker, Ben Welden, Bennie Bartlett, Tom Kennedy, William Ruhl.* Dir.: William Beaudine. Pro.: Jan Grippo. (Pathe.) Rel.: July 19.

Joe Palooka In The Knockout. A further episode in the adventures of the comic strip hero. Cast: *Leon Errol, Joe Kirkwood, Morris Carnovsky, Elyse Knox, Billy House, Trudy Marshall, Marc Lawrence, Whitford Kane, Benny Baker, Donald McBride, Danny Morton, Vince Barnett, Eddie Gribbon, Michael Mark, Sarah Padden, Clarence Muse, James Flavin, Chester Clute, Suni Chorre, Charles Smith, Jay Norris, Jack Roper, Ray Walker, Cathy Carter, Sam Hayes.* Dir.: Reginald Le Borg. Pro.: Hal E. Chester. (Pathe.) Rel.: Oct. 4.

Journey Into Yesterday. (Original title Portrait of Hildegarde. Post-war story about a British Army Major who becomes interested in a portrait of a girl (*Mai Zetterling*) and whose enquiries about it lead him into a strange and mysterious quest in Germany. Rest of cast: *Robert Beatty, Guy Rolfe, Herbert Lom, Patrick Holt, Arnold Marle, Sybilla Binder, Thora Hird, Gerard Heinz, Philo Hauser, Yvonne Owen, Cyril Chamberlain, Michael Hordern, Ernest Thesiger, Arthur Hambling, John Blythe, Dennis Harkin, Lucille Rath, Peter Murray, Richard Molinas, Dennis Vance, George Thorpe, Eric Pohlmann, Nelly Arno, Anthony Steel, Carl Jaffe, Renee Goddard, Liselotte Kristian, Gordon Bell, Dorothy Glade, Joseph Plaut, Oscar Ebelsbacher, Christina Forbes, Betty Lynne, Frank Ling, Henrick Jacobson, Charles Rolfe, Egan Wayne, Ralph de Pomerai, Hugo Schuster, Sam Kydd, Paul Hansard, Jan Stachow, Bernard Rebel, Willoughby Grey, Lionel Grose, Eric Messiter, Dandy Nichols, Arthur Young.* Dir.: Terence Fisher. Pro.: Anthony Darnborough. (Gainsborough.) Rel.: Dec. 6.

K **Killer At Large.** Another ace reporter uncovers another racket. Cast: *Robert Lowery, Anabel Shaw, Charles Evans, Frank Ferguson, George Lynn, Dick Rich, Ann Staunton, Leonard Penn.* Dir.: William Beaudine. Pro.: Buck Gottlieb. (Pathe.) Rel.: Aug. 30.

Killer McCoy. Extremely good boxing film with *Mickey Rooney* as the newsboy who fights his way to the championship through all the usual pitfalls and temptations. There's even the last-minute change of heart in the ring, when *Rooney* decides *not* to throw the fight as planned. Rest of cast: *Brian Donlevy, Ann Blyth, James Dunn, Tom Tully, Sam Levene, Walter Sande, Mickey Knox, James Bell, Gloria Holden, Eve March, June Story.* Dir.: Roy Rowland. Pro.: Sam Zimbalist. (Metro-Goldwyn-Mayer.) Rel.: Oct. 18.

Kilroy Was Here. Former infant prodigies *Jackie Cooper* and *Jackie Coogan* as ex-G.I. friends. Rest of cast: *Wanda McKay, Frank Jenks, Norman Phillips, Barton Yarborough, Therese Lyon, Raymond Largay, Rand Brooks, Phil Arnold, Joe Forte.* Dir.: Phil Karlson. Pro.: Dick Irving Hyland and Sid Luft. (Pathe.) Rel.: Oct. 4.

Kiss of Death. First-rate, thrilling modern gangster story about an ex-criminal (*Victor Mature*) who, because his wife is having an affaire with one of his former associates, turns "squealer" and then has to take the consequences. Based on facts, photographed in the actual streets and buildings involved. Rest of cast: *Brian Donlevy, Coleen Gray, Richard Widmark, Taylor Holmes, Howard Smith, Karl Malden, Anthony Ross, Mildred Dunnock, Millard Mitchell, Temple Texas, J. Scott Smart.* Dir.: Henry Hathaway. Pro.: Fred Kohlmar. (20th Cent. Fox.) Rel.: Sept. 20.

L **Lady of Deceit.** Murder mystery with *Claire Trevor* mixed up in two deaths. Somewhat involved. Rest of cast: *Lawrence Tierney, Walter Slezak, Phillip Terry, Audrey Long, Elisha Cook, Jr., Isabel Jewell, Esther Howard, Kathryn Card, Tony Barrett, Grandon Rhodes.* Dir.: Robert Wise. Pro.: Herman Schlom. (R.K.O. Radio.) Rel.: Aug. 9.

Land of the Lawless. Western. Cast: *Johnny Mack Brown, Raymond Hatton, Christine McIntyre, Tristram Coffin, Juno Harrison, Marshall Reed, L. Stanford Jolley, Steve Clark, Edmund Cobb, Roy Butler, Cactus Mack, Cary Garrett.* (Pathe.) Rel.: Dec. 13.

Letter From An Unknown Woman. Tragic story of a great and unrequited love, set in old Vienna. A gaslit tear-jerker based on the Stefan Zweig story, with *Joan Fontaine* as the adolescent girl who adores pianist *Louis Jourdan,* spends a single night with him, has his child and then suffers steadily about it all; right to the end. Rest of cast: *Mady Christians, Marcel Journet.* Dir.: *Max Ophuls.* Pro.: John Houseman. (Universal-International.) Rel.: Late 1948 or early 1949.

Life With Father. Technicolored screen adaptation of the famous and long-running stage play of the same title. A great deal of the fun rises from the fact that Mama (*Irene Dunne*), after having four of his children, discovers that Father (*William Powell*) has never been baptised ! Quiet, amusing guying of the gaslit era. Rest of cast: *Elisabeth Taylor, Edmund Gwenn, Zasu Pitts, Jimmy Lydon, Emma Dunn, Moroni Olsen, Elizabeth Risdon, Derek Scott, Johnny Calkins, Martin Milner, Heather Wilde, Monte Blue, Mary Field, Queenie Leonard, Nancy Evans, Clara Blandick, Frank Elliott.* Dir.: *Michael Curtiz.* Pro.: Oscar Serlin. (Warner.) Rel.: Oct. 11.

London Belongs To Me. The story of a silly and romantically-minded young crook who loses his nerve and is tried and convicted of murder; also of the other amusing and pathetic characters who live in No.10 Dulcimer Street. Adapted from the novel by Norman Collins. A quite outstanding, brilliant picture, thanks to a superb script, realistic dialogue and first-class acting. A serious theme but, owing to the satirical treatment, also a richly amusing movie. Cast: *Richard Attenborough, Alastair Sim, Stephen Murray, Fay Compton, Wylie Watson, Susan Shaw, Ivy St. Helier, Joyce Carey, Andrew Crawford, Eleanor Summerfield, Gladys Henson, Hugh Griffith, Arthur Howard, Maurice Denham, Jack McKnaughton, Hatton Duprez, Ivor Barnard, Kenneth Downey, Cecil Trouncer, Lionel Gross, Russell Waters, Michael Kent, Basil Cunard, Cyril Chamberlain, Edward Evans, John Salew, Henry Edwards, Fabia Drake, Alexis France, Myrette Morven, Aubrey Dexter, Henry Hewitt, J. H. Roberts, Wensley Pithey, Stanley Rose, John Boxer, Manville Tarrant, George Cross, Owen Reynolds, Sydney Tafler, D. A. Mehan, Susan Buret, Frank Ling, Alan Saynes.* Dir.: Sidney Gilliatt. Pro.: Frank Launder and Sidney Gilliatt. (Individual.) Rel.: Sept. 13.

Lone Wolf in London. Lone Wolf *Gerald Mohr* chases the mystery of the twin diamonds, The Eyes of the Nile. Rest of cast: *Nancy Saunders, Eric Blore, Evelyn Ankers, Richard Fraser, Queenie Leonard, Alan Napier, Denis Green.* Dir.: Leslie Goodwins. Pro.: Ted Richmond. (Columbia.) Rel.: Aug. 2.

Look Before You Love. *Margaret Lockwood* marries polished crook *Griffith Jones,* but eventually gives up her efforts to reform him and turns to honest, wealthy financier *Norman Wooland.* Rest of cast: *Phyllis Stanley, Frederick Piper, Maurice Denham, Michael Medwin, Bruce Seton.* Dir.: Harold Huth. Pro.: John Corfield and Harold Huth. (Huth-Corfield.) Rel.: Nov. 8.

The Lost Moment. Somewhat arty, long, romantic melodrama which brings love, murder and madness together in a Venetian mansion in the year 1900. Cast: *Susan Hayward, Agnes Moorehead, Robert Cummings, Joan Lorring, Eduardo Ciannelli, John Archer, Frank Puglia, Minerva Urecal, William Edmunds.* Dir.: Martin Gabel. Pro.: Walter Wanger. (Universal International-Wanger.) Rel: Late 1948 or early 1949.

Lulu Belle. *Dorothy Lamour,* as 1905 cafe singer, works her way up the ladder with the assistance of progressively affluent males. From the Belasco stage play which originally helped Mae West to stardom. Rest of cast: *George Montgomery, Albert Dekker, Otto Kruger, Glenda Farrell, Greg McClure, Charlotte*

Wynters, Addison Richards, William Haade, Ben Erway, Clancy Cooper. Dir.: Leslie Fenton. Pro.: Benedict Bogeaus. (Columbia-Bogeaus.) Rel.: Nov. 8.

The Mating of Milly. *Evelyn Keyes* showing *Glenn Ford* that he's no match for her when she decides he should be the father of her son. Comedy. Rest of cast: *Ron Randell, Willard Parker, Jimmy Hunt, Mabel Paige, Virginia Brissac, Patsy Creighton, Tom Stevenson.* Pro.: Casey Robinson. (Columbia.) Rel.: Aug. 23.

The Miracle of the Bells. Based on the novel by Russell Janney, this is the story of a Hollywood star who wanted to be buried in the small town of her birth, the kindly local priest who arranges that this shall be done, and the Hollywood producer whom only a miracle can convince. New Italian star *Valli* plays the girl, *Fred McMurray* her publicity agent secretly in love with her, *Frank Sinatra* the priest and *Lee J. Cobb* the producer. Rest of cast: *Veronica Pataky, Philip Ahn, Harold Vermilyea.* Dir.: Irving Pichel. Pro.: Jesse L. Lasky and Walter MacEwen. (R.K.O. Radio.) Rel.: Late 1948.

Mother Wore Tights. Lush, Technicolored musical along familiar lines, set at the turn of the century and giving *Betty Grable* one of the best roles of her career. Rest of cast: *Dan Dailey, Mona Freeman, Connie Marshall, Vanessa Brown, Sara Allgood, Robert Arthur, Sig Ruman, Lee Patrick, William Frawley, Ruth Nelson.* Dir.: Walter Lang. Pro.: Lamar Trotti. (20th Century-Fox.) Rel.: Late 1948 or early 1949.

Mr. Ashton Was Indiscreet. Called in America "*The Senator Was Indiscreet*" this is a comedy about a Senator who wanted to become President and attempted it the easy way, by threatening to make public the diary about the indiscretions of the big shots of his Party which he has been keeping for 30 years! The role of the Senator is played up to the hilt by *William Powell.* Rest of cast: *Ella Raines, Arleen Whelan, Peter Lind Hayes, Ray Collins, Allen Jenkins, Hans Conried, Whitney Bissell, Milton Parsons, Charles D. Brown, Francis Pierlot, Oliver Blake, Iron Eyes Cody, Chief Thundercloud, Chief Yowlache, Cynthia Corley.* Dir.: Geo. S. Kaufman. Pro.: Nunnally Johnson (Universal-International) Rel.: Not fixed at press-time.

Mr. Perrin and Mr. Traill. A story of two house-masters at a public school; one (*Marius Goring*) a frustrated middle-aged, shy bachelor, and the other (*David Farrar*) young, ex-Army and full of drive. The climax of their clash comes when they both realise they are in love with the school nurse (*Greta Gynt*). Rest of cast: *Raymond Huntley, Edward Chapman, Ralph Truman, Lloyd Pearson, Archie Harradine, Maurice Jones, Mary Jerrold, Viola Lyel, May McDonald, Pat Nye, Finlay Currie, Donald Barclay, Brendan Clegg, John Campbell, David Liney, David Spenser, Cavan Malone, Brian McDermot, Roy Sargent, Sheila Huntington, Howard Douglas, Roddy Hughes, John Schofield, John Warren.* Dir.: Laurence Huntington. Pro.: Alexander Galperson. (Two Cities.) Rel.: Sept. 27.

My Brother's Keeper. Quite outstanding British picture; the realistic, exciting story of a man hunt. Two convicts, one a boy, the other an old lag, jump their way to escape, handcuffed together, on the way to prison. Eventually they separate, the boy gives himself up, the old lag goes on to murder and final death in a bold attempt to escape again when he is at last cornered by the police. Brilliantly casual treatment, deft touches of humour and a wonderful, constant atmosphere of tension. The film gave chances to new director, new technicians and new players. First-class acting; an outstanding performance by *Jack Warner* as the old lag, brilliant work by *Jane Hylton* (as his girl friend) and *George Cole* (as the boy criminal). Rest of cast: *Bill Owen, David Tomlinson, Yvonne Owen, Raymond Lovell, Beatrice Varley, Amy Veness, Brenda Bruce, Susan Shaw, John Boxer, Fred Groves, Garry Marsh, Wilfred Hyde-White, Arthur Hambling, Frederick Piper, Valentine Dyall, George Merritt, Maurice Denham, Jack Raine.* Dir.: Alfred Roome. Pro.: Anthony Darnborough. (Gainsborough.) Rel.: Aug. 9.

My Dog Rusty. Untruthful little boy tells the truth, saves the local Mayor from a scandal. Cast: *Ted Donaldson, Ann Doran, John Litel, Mona Barrie.* Dir.: Lew Landers. Pro.: Wallace MacDonald. (Columbia.) Rel.: Sept. 13.

My Girl Tisa. Sometimes touching, sometimes humdrum and generally sentimental tale of a foreign immigrant girl who comes to New York's East Side at the beginning of the 20th Century. Cast: *Lilli Palmer, Sam Wanamaker, Akim Tamiroff, Alan Hale, Hugo Haas, Gale Robbins, Stella Adler, Benny Baker, Sumner Getchell, Sid Tomack, John Qualen, Tom Dillon, Sidney Blackmer, Fritz Feld, John Banner.* Dir.: Elliott Nugent. (Warner.) Rel.: Nov. 15.

My Own True Love. *Phyllis Calvert* went to America to star in this picture, a Hollywood made romance set in post-war London, with *Miss Calvert* as a member of the A.T.S. Rest of cast: *Melvyn Douglas, Wanda Hendrix, Philip Friend, Phyllis Morris.* Dir.: Compton Bennett. Pro.: Val Lewton. (Paramount.) Rel.: Late 1948 or early 1949.

My Sister And I. Melodramatic story about a wealthy widow who for years believes her husband loved her, only to find out that the paragon had a passion for her sister, to whom he wrote even on their honeymoon and to whom he, later, gave a child. Cast: *Sally Ann Howes, Dermot Walsh, Martita Hunt, Barbara Mullen, Patrick Holt, Hazel Court, Joan Rees, Jane Hylton, Michael Medwin, Rory McDermott, Hugh Miller, Ian Wilson, Niall Lawlor, Elizabeth Sydney, Jack Vyvyan, Helen Goss, Stewart Rome, Olwyn Brooks, Wilfred Caithness, John Miller, Amy Dalby, James Knight, Barbara Leake, Diana Dors.* Dir. and Pro.: Harold Huth. (Burnham.) Rel.: Aug. 7.

Mystery in Mexico. Mystery in that country with *William Lundigan* solving it. Made in Mexico. Rest of cast: *Jacqueline White, Ricardo Cortez, Tony Barrett, Jacqueline Dalya, Walter Reed, Jose Torvay, Maime Jimenez, Antonio Frausto, Dolores Camerillo, Eduardo Casado, Thalia Draper.* Dir.: Robert Wise. Pro.: Sid Rogell. (R.K.O. Radio.) Rel.: Late 1948.

My Wild Irish Rose. Familiar but pleasing musical, a fictional biography of a vaudeville singer of the 1900's. Nostalgic and Technicolored. Cast: *Dennis Morgan, Arlene Dahl, Andrea King, Alan Hale, George Tobias, George O'Brien, Ben Blue, Sara Allgood, William Frawley, Don McGuire, Charles Irwin, Clifton Young, Paul Stanton, George Cleveland, Oscar O'Shea, Ruby Dandridge, Grady Sutton, William Davidson, Douglas Wood, Charles Marsh, Igor Dega, Pierre Andre, The Three Dunhills, Lou Wills, Jr.* Dir.: David Butler. (Warner.) Rel.: Dec. 27.

The Naked City. Tremendously effective, completely realistic whodunnit; the last film to be made prior to his death by columnist, film writer-producer Mark Hellinger. It is the story of a murder, the sifting of clues and following up of leads by the police, and the breathless, painfully exciting climax when the man-hunt goes into full cry and the murderer is chased to his death among the girders of the Brooklyn Bridge. Made with documentary casualness, underwritten and underplayed, photographed in the buildings and streets of New York and always bearing a completely authentic air. Beautifully acted by *Barry*

Don McGuire, Arlene Dahl and Dennis Morgan in MY WILD IRISH ROSE—Warner.

Coleen Gray and Tyrone Power in NIGHT-MARE ALLEY—20th Century-Fox.

Fitzgerald as the detective, *Don Taylor* as his assistant and *Howard Duff, Dorothy Hart, Ted de Corsia, House Jameson, Anne Sargent, Adelaide Kleine, Grover Burgess, Tom Pedi, Enid Markey, Frank Conroy.* Dir.: Jules Dassin. Pro.: Mark Hellinger. (Universal-International.) Rel.: Aug. 16.

Night Has A Thousand Eyes. Mystery thriller with *Edward G. Robinson* as a mental wizard predicting the day and hour of lovely *Gail Russell's* death. Rest of cast: *John Lund, William Demarest, Virginia Bruce.* Dir.: John Farrow. Pro.: Endre Bohem. (Paramount.) Rel.: Oct. 4.

Nightmare Alley. *Tyrone Power* in a somewhat emasculated screen adaptation of the William Lindsay Gresham novel about a young man who rises to the top, and falls again to the bottom, of the circus sideshow business. Rest of cast: *Joan Blondell, Coleen Gray, Helen Walker, Taylor Holmes, Mike Mazurki, Ian Keith, Julia Dean.* Dir.: Edmund Goulding. Pro.: George Jessel. (20th Century-Fox.) Rel.: Sept. 13.

No Orchids for Miss Blandish. Somewhat indifferent film of the best-selling James Hadley Chase gangster story about a most unpleasant gangster, Slim, and the girl—Miss Blandish—he " snatches " and then falls in love with ! Cast: *Jack La Rue* (Slim), *Linden Travers* (Miss Blandish), *Hugh McDermott, Walter Crisham, Leslie Bradley, Zoe Gail, Charles Goldner, MacDonald Parke, Percy Marmont, Lilly Molner, Frances Marsden, Danny Green, Jack Lester, Bart Norman, Bill O'Connor, Irene Prador, Michael Balfour, Gibb McLaughlin, John McLaren, Sidney James, Richard Nelson, Annette Simmonds, Jack Durant, Halama and Konarski, Toy and Wing.* Dir.: St. John L. Clowes. Pro.: Oswald Mitchell. (Renown.) Rel.: Indefinite.

Noose. Film of the Richard Llewellyn play about London rackets and racketeers. Actually another British gangster movie. Cast: *Carole Landis, Joseph Calleia, Derek Farr, Stanley Holloway, Nigel Patrick, Ruth Nixon, Carol Van Derman, Hay Petrie, John Slater, Leslie Bradley, Reginald Tate, Edward Rigby, John Salew, Robert Adair, Uriel Porter, Ella Retford, Brenda Hogan, Sidney Monckton, Howard Douglas, Michael Golden, W. E. Hodge, Michael Brennan, Arthur Lovegrove, John Harvey, Michael Ripper, Philip Godfrey, Monti de Lyle, Dennis Harkin, Diana Hope, Arthur Gomez, Kenneth Buckley, Ben Williams, Vi Kaley, John Martell, Ernest Metcalfe, Maria Barry, Ronald Boyer & Jeanne Ravel, Olive Lucius.* Dir.: Edmond T. Greville. Pro.: Edward Dryhurst. (Pathe.) Rel.: Nov. 15.

No Room at the Inn. Film of long-running stage play by Joan Temple about a gin-soaked old harridan who—for the money—takes in some child evacuees. Cast includes *Freda Jackson* (who created the role on the stage), *Hermione Baddeley, Joan Dowling, Nial McGinnis, Joy Shelton.* Dir.: Dan Birt. Pro.: Joan Foxwell. (British-National-Pathe.) Rel.: Nov. 22.

O **Oliver Twist.** One of the finest British films for a very long time ; better even than the same production company's first Dickens classic, " Great Expectations." Brilliantly directed, acted and produced. From its dark, stormy opening, through the black deeds of

the underworld it pictures, to the final scene when for the first time the sun shines out brightly, this is a poem in celluloid, a composition of inspired brilliance. Superb performances from *Robert Newton* as Bill Sykes, *Alec Guinness* as Fagin and *Kay Walsh* as Nancy. And as the boy who dared to ask for more, wan, wistful and frightened-looking little *John Howard Davies* is ideal. Rest of cast : *Francis L. Sullivan, Henry Stephenson, Mary Clare, Josephine Stuart, Kathleen Harrison, Amy Veness, W. G. Fay, Maurice Denham, Frederick Lloyd, Ivor Barnard, Deidre Doyle, Edie Martin, Fay Middleton, Diana Dors, Michael Dear, Graveley Edwards, Peter Bull, John Potter, Maurice Jones, Henry Edwards, Ralph Truman, Anthony Newley, Hattie Jacques, Betty Paul, Kenneth Downy, Gibb McLaughlin.* Dir.: David Lean. Pro.: Ronald Neame. (Cineguild.) Rel.: Oct. 25.

Once A Jolly Swagman. The story of a speedway rider before, during and after the war, with a factual background of the track. Cast: *Dirk Bogarde, Bonar Colleano, Bill Owen, Renee Asherson, Sidney James, Patric Doonan, Thora Hird, James Hayter, Moira Lister, Stuart Linsell, Dudley Jones, Sandra Dorne, Cyril Chamberlain, Anthony Oliver, Graham Doody, Cyril Cusack, June Bardsley, Pauline Jameson, Betty Cooper, Michael Kent, Russell Waters, Freddy Knight, Joyce Tyler, Jill Allan, Jennifer Jayne.* Dir.: Jack Lee. Pro.: Derek Twist. (Wessex.) Rel.: Nov. 29.

P **Paleface.** *Bob Hope* has *Jane* (Outlaw) *Russell* to accompany him in his trip to the very wild West in 1870. Hope plays a dentist, *Miss Russell* plays Calamity Jane. Rest of cast: *Robert Armstrong, Iris Adrian, Robert Watson, Jack Searl, Joseph Vitale, Charles Trowbridge, Clem Bevans, Jeff York, Stanley Andrews, Wade Crosby, Chief Yowlachie, Iron Eyes Cody, John Maxwell, Tom Kennedy, Henry Brandon, Francis J. McDonald, Frank Hagney, Skelton Knaggs Olin Howland, George Chandler, Nestor Paiva.* Dir.: Norman Z. McLeod. Pro.: Robert L. Welch. (Paramount.) Rel.: Late 1948.

The Paradine Case. Alfred Hitchcock directed this story of the 1946 murder trial at the Old Bailey ; about a blind V.C. who dies of poisoning, his wife, who is accused of the crime, and of the defending counsel, who becomes more than casually interested in his client. Cast : *Gregory Peck, Ann Todd, Charles Laughton, Charles Coburn, Ethel Barrymore, Louis Jourdan, Valli, Joan Tetzel, Leo. G. Carroll, John Goldsworthy, Lester Matthews, Pat Aherne, Colin Hunter, Isobel Elsom.* Dir.: Alfred Hitchcock. Pro.: David O. Selznick. (Selznick-International.) Rel.: Late 1948.

Penny and The Pownall Case. Detective Inspector *Ralph Michael,* in unravelling a murder case, uncovers a plot for the escape of German war criminals. First of the Rank Highbury-made features. Rest of cast : *Peggy Evans, Christopher Lee, Diana Dors, Frederick Piper, Olaf Pooley, Ethel Coleridge, Sam Costa, Dennis Vance, Shaun Noble, Philip Saville, John Lorrell, Peter Madren, Duncan Carse.* Dir.: Slim Hand. Pro.: John Croydon. (Highbury.) Rel.: July 26.

Philo Vance Returns. Thriller. Mr. Vance solving another murder. Cast : *William Wright, Terry Austin, Leon Belasco, Clara Blandick, Ramsey Ames, Damian O'Flynn, Frank Wilcox, Iris Adrian, Ann Staunton, Tim Murdock, Mary Scott.* Dir.: William Beaudine. Pro.: Howard Welsch. (Pathe.) Rel.: Late 1948.

Philo Vance's Secret Mission. Philo discovers why one publishing firm's partner kills another. Cast : *Alan Curtis, Sheila Ryan, Tala Birell, Frank Jenks, James Bell, Frank Fenton, Paul Maxey, Kenneth Farrell.* Dir.: Reginald Le Borg. Pro.: Howard Welsch. (Pathe.) Rel.: Aug. 23.

The Pirate. The first big, spectacular Technicolored musical to be shown in England since the tax was imposed ; and the best of its kind in ages. Fast-moving, sparkling, amusing, with some amazing dancing by Gene Kelly and good Cole Porter songs by Judy Garland. Rest of cast : *Walter Slezak, Gladys Cooper, George Zucco, Reginald Owen.* Dir.: Vincente Minnelli. Pro.: Arthur Freed. (Metro-Goldwyn-Mayer.) Rel.: Oct. 11.

Port Said. American author *William Bishop* helps the police solve several murders in the unsavoury Eastern port. Rest of cast : *Gloria Henry, William Bishop, Steven Geray, Edgar Barrier, Richard Hale, Ian Macdonald, Blanche Zohar, Robin Hughes, Jay Novello.* Dir.: Reginald Le Borg. Pro.: Wallace Macdonald. (Columbia.) Rel.: Sept. 20.

Q **Quartette.** Lavish Sydney Box portmanteau production with four separate episodes based on four short Somerset Maugham stories. First story is **The Kite,** which is all about a strange family who have a weakness for such toys. Cast : *Mervyn Johns, Hermione Baddeley, Susan Shaw, George Cole, David Cole, Frederick Leister, George Merritt, Cyril Chamberlain.* Dir.: Arthur Crabtree. Pro.: Anthony Darnborough. The second episode is **The Colonel's Lady,** a satirical comedy. Cast : *Cecil Parker, Nora Swinburne, Linden Travers, Clive Morton, Cyril Raymond, Ernest Thesiger, Harcourt Williams, Felix Aylmer, J. H. Roberts, Mary Eaton, Lyn Evans, Wilfred Hyde-White, Claud Allister, Margaret Withers, Yvonne Owen, Margaret Thorburn.* Dir.: Ken Annakin. Pro.: Anthony Darnborough. Third episode, **Alien Corn,** is about a young man who wants to be a great pianist but just isn't any good. Cast : *Dirk Bogarde, Francoise Rosay, Irene Browne, Raymond Lovell, George Thorpe, Honor Blackman, Mary Hinton, Maurice Denham, James Hayter, Russell Barry, Henry Morrell, Molly Mainwaring, Cecil Paul, Harman Phelps, Marcel Poncin, Ben Williams.* Dir.: Harold French. Pro.: Anthony Darnborough. Last episode, **The Facts of Life,** is about a young man who went to Monte Carlo and, ignoring his father's advice not to gamble, made himself a fortune. Cast : *Basil Radford, Naunton Wayne, Mai Zetterling, Angela Baddeley, Nigel Buchanan, James Robertson-Justice, Jack Watling, Jack Raine, Ian Fleming.* Dir.: Ralph Smart. Pro.: Anthony Darnborough. (Gainsborough.) Rel.: Nov. 22

R **Raiders of the South.** *Johnny Mack Brown v.* The Carpetbaggers. Western. Rest of cast : *Evelyn Brent, Raymond Hatton, Reno Blair, Marshall Reed, John Hamilton, John Merton, Edwin Parker, Frank LaRue, Ted Adams, Pierce Lyden, Cactus Mack, Curt Barrett and The Trailsmen,* Dir.: Lambert Hillyer. Pro.: Scott R. Dunlap. (Pathe.) Rel.: Late 1948.

The Red Shoes. A Technicolored story of the ballet, made by Michael Powell and Emeric Pressburger, which contains an actual full-length ballet (based on the old Hans Andersen fairy story), which is technically one of the most brilliant pieces of filmcraft of the year. Otherwise the film is interesting, though long and sometimes thin in story. It's the old theme of love *v.* career, in this case complicated by the fact that both lovers are artistes who really love their work. Ballerina *Moira Shearer* (on the screen for the first time), looks lovely and dances exquisitely, assisted by *Leonide Massine* and *Robert Helpmann.* Rest of cast : *Anton Walbrook, Marius Goring, Jean Short, Gordon Littman, Julia Lang, Bill Shine, Austin Trevor, Esmond Knight, Eric Berry, Irene Browne, Ludmilla Tcherina, Jerry Verno, Albert Basserman, Derek Elphinstone, Madame Rambert, Joy Rawlins, Marcel Poncin, Michel Bazalgette, Yvonne Andre, Hay Petrie.* Written, directed and produced by Michael Powell and Emeric Pressburger. (Archers.) Rel.: Sept. 6.

Relentless. *Robert Young,* as a wandering cowboy, finds adventure and romance (*Marguerite Chapman*) in them thar Technicolored hills. . . . Rest of cast : *Willard Parker, Akim Tamiroff, Barton MacLane, Mike Mazurki, Robert Barrat, Clem Bevans, Frank Fenton, Hank Patterson, Paul Burns, Emmett Lynn, Will Wright.* Dir.: George Sherman. Pro.: Eugene B. Rodney. (Columbia.) Rel.: Nov. 1.

Ride the Pink Horse. Tough, intelligent movie about a war veteran who comes to a small New Mexican town during fiesta time determined on blackmail, and revenge for his murdered friend. A brilliant acting and directing performance by Robert Montgomery; excellent work from *Wanda Hendrix* as the little Indian girl who adopts him, *Thomas Gomez* as Pancho, who befriends him, and *Bill Retz,* a kindly old detective. A most interesting picture. Rest of cast : *Rita Conde, Iris Flores, Grandon Rhodes, Tito Renaldo, Richard Gaines, Andrea King, Martin Garralaga, Edward Earle*

Harold Goodwin, Maria Cortez, Fred Clark. Dir.: Robert Montgomery. Pro.: Joan Harrison. (Universal-International.) Rel.: Aug. 16.

S The Sainted Sisters. *Veronica Lake* and *Joan Caulfield*, two lovely crooks with £5,000 hot money in their pockets, descend on small-town philosopher *Barry Fitzgerald* and learn from him the old lesson that in the end the Saint is happier than the Sinner ! Rest of cast : *George Reeves, William Demarest, Beulah Bondi, Chill Wills, Dorothy Adams, Kathryn Card, Eddie Parks, Jimmy Hunt.* Dir.: William Russell. Pro.: Richard Maibaum. (Paramount.) Rel.: Late 1948 or early 1949.

Saraband For Dead Lovers. Period piece. The story of Sophie-Dorothea, a girl forced for political reasons into marriage with George Louis of Hanover, later King George I of England. Cast : *Stewart Granger, Joan Greenwood, Flora Robson, Francoise Rosay, Frederick Valk, Peter Bull, Anthony Quayle, Michael Gough, Megs Jenkins, Jill Balcon, David Horne, Mercia Swinburne, Cecil Trouncer, Noel Howlett, Barbara Leake, Miles Malleson, Anthony Lang, Rosemary Lang, Edward Sinclair, Allan Jeayes, Aubrey Mallalieu, Guy Rolfe, Margaret Vines, Peter George, W. E. Holloway, Myles Eason, Victor Adams, Peter Albrecht, Janet Howe.* Dir.: Basil Dearden. Pro : Michael Balcon. (Ealing.) Rel.: Oct. 4.

Sealed Verdict. Another post-war drama, set in Germany with an American attorney trying to discover which—if any—of six Nazis condemned to death is innocent. Cast : *Ray Milland, Florence Marly, Broderick Crawford, John Ridgely, Ludwig Donath.* Dir.: Lewis Allen. Pro.: Robert Fellows. (Paramount.) Rel.: Late 1948 or early 1949.

Secret Beyond the Door. *Michael Redgrave* went to Hollywood to share this Fritz Lang thriller with *Joan Bennett.* He plays a "psychological murderer" while Miss Bennett plays the girl who woos him from such a hobby by her love. Always tense, sometimes exciting. Rest of cast : *Anne Revere, Barbara O'Neil, Natalie Schafer, Anabel Shaw, Rosa Rey, James Seay, Mark Dennis.* Dir. and Pro.: Fritz Lang. (Universal-International.) Rel.: Late 1948 or early 1949.

Shaggy. Another sentimental story of a boy and a dog saved from death. This time in Cinecolor. Cast : *Brenda Joyce, George Nokes, Robert Shayne, Ralph Sanford, Jody Gilbert, Ian McDonald, Alex Frazer, Don White.* Dir.: Robert E. Tansey. Pro.: William Pine, William Thomas. (Paramount.) Rel.: Aug. 16.

The Sign of the Ram. Mediocre little film about the trouble caused by a woman's jealousy ; interesting in that it brings back to the screen lovely little *Susan Peters* who, victim of a hunting accident, is doomed to spend the rest of her life in a wheel chair. She plays a part of such a woman in the movie ! Rest of cast : *Alexander Knox, Phyllis Thaxter, Peggy Ann Garner, Ron Randell, Dame May Whitty, Allene Roberts, Ross Ford, Diana Douglas, Margaret Tracy, Paul Scardon, Gerald Hamer, Doris Lloyd.* Dir.: John Sturges. Pro.: Irving Cummings, Jnr. (Columbia.) Rel.: Aug. 2.

Silver River. *Errol Flynn,* thrown out of the Union Army during the civil war goes out West and unscrupulously climbs to great power by gambling, blackmail and other strictly illegal means. He even murders (if indirectly) her husband, in order to get *Ann Sheridan.* Rest of cast : *Thomas Mitchell, Bruce Bennett, Tom D'Andrea, Barton MacLane, Monte Blue, Jonathan Hale, Alan Bridge, Arthur Space, Art Baker, Joseph Crehan.* Dir.: Raoul Walsh. Pro.: Owen Crump. (Warner.) Rel.: Nov. 15.

Sitting Pretty. Consistently amusing, often quite uproariously funny comedy about a young couple (*Maureen O'Hara* and *Robert Young*) who advertise for a resident nurse and, somewhat to their bewilderment, get suave, witty, baby-hating *Clifton Webb,* self-styled genius who proceeds to demonstrate he doesn't underestimate himself. His methods with the children are drastic, but effective—his methods with everyone else quite as drastic and quite as effective. *Webb* is superb. Rest of cast : *Richard Haydn, Louise Allbritton, Randy Stuart,*

Ed Begley, Larry Olsen, John Russell, Betty Ann Lynn, Willard Robertson, Anthony Sydes, Roddy McCaskill, Grayce Hampton, Cara Williams, Marion Marshall, Charles Arnt, Ken Christy, Ann Shoemaker, Minerva Urecal, Mira McKinney, Sid Saylor, Ruth Warren, Isabel Randolph, Ellen Lowe, Dave Morris, Anne O'Neal, Albin Robeling, Josephine Whittle, Mary Field, Billy Wayne, Charles Owens, Robert Tidwell, Iris James.* Dir.: Walter Lang. Pro.: Samuel G. Engel. (20th Century-Fox.) Rel.: July 19.

Sleeping Car To Trieste. Remake of the old British thriller " *Rome Express,*" about the adventures of a group of characters making the journey from Paris to Trieste. There's murder, romance and tragedy en route. Cast : *Jean Kent, Albert Lieven, Derrick de Marney, Rona Anderson, David Tomlinson, Paul Dupuis, Bonar Colleano, Alan Wheatley, Leslie Weston, Finlay Currie, Hugh Burden, Michael Ward, David Hutcheson, Jefferson Searles, Coco Aslan, George de Warfaz, Claude Larue, Zena Marshall.* Dir.: John Paddy Carstairs. Pro.: George Brown. (Two Cities.) Rel.: Nov. 8.

The Small Voice. Dramatic story set in the lonely Welsh hills, where a man and his wife take to their house some men they rescue from a road crash and then find they have picked up some dangerous and unscrupulous criminals. Cast : *Valerie Hobson, James Donald, Joan Young, Harold Keel, Michael Balfour, David Greene, Glyn Dearman, Angela Foulds.* Dir.: Fergus McDonnell. Pro.: Anthony Havelock-Allan. (British Lion.) Rel.: Late 1948.

Smart Woman. Crime melo. *Constance Bennett* as criminal lawyer, *Brian Aherne* a prosecutor in love with her but resolutely intent upon convicting her clients, *Otto Kruger* as a corrupt district attorney not above committing a murder and *Barry Sullivan* as a criminal guilty of every crime in the book except the one for which he goes to trial. Rest of cast : *Michael O'Shea, James Gleason, Isobel Elsom, Richard Lyon, Selena Royle, Taylor Holmes, John Litel, Nita Hunter, Iris Adrian, Willie Best.* Dir.: Edward A. Blatt. Pro.: Hal E. Chester. (Pathe.) Rel.: Aug. 9.

So Evil My Love. Highly polished, beautifully produced and excellently acted gas-lit Period Piece from the Joseph Shearing story which never rings true. But in the role of the Missionary Widow who comes back to England to fall in love with, and into the clutches of, unmoral painter *Ray Milland, Ann Todd* gives a most tender, moving and altogether superb performance. Also good are *Geraldine Fitzgerald* as the old school friend, *Raymond Huntley* as the stern husband, *Moira Lister* as Millard's girl-friend and *Raymond Lovell* as his companion in crime. Also in the cast : *Martita Hunt, Leo. G. Carroll, Muriel Aked, Roderick Lovell,* and *Finlay Currie.* Dir.: Lewis Allen. Pro.: Hal Wallis. (Paramount British.) Rel.: Aug. 9.

Spring in Park Lane. The third Herbert Wilcox film to co-star *Anna Neagle* with *Michael Wilding,* and far and away the best of the trio. Charming, thoroughly amusing light comedy with excellent lines, funny situations, delightful performances and rich production. For these qualities one easily overlooks the silly story about an Honourable masquerading as a butler and falling in love with the lady of the house. British comedy that is really amusing. *Tom Walls* and *Peter Graves* excellent in supporting roles. Rest of cast : *Marjorie Fielding, Nicholas Phipps, G. H. Mulcaster, Josephine Fitzgerald, Nigel Patrick, Lana Morris, Catherine Paul, H. R. Hignett, Cyril Conway, Tom Walls, Jr.* Dir. and Pro.: Herbert Wilcox. (British Lion.) Rel.: Sept. 13.

T That Hagen Girl. *Shirley Temple* finds that a doubtful parentage can lead to a great deal of trouble in a small town, even in these days. In fact, it brings her to the edge of suicide before she finds eventual love and happiness. Rest of cast : *Ronald Reagan, Rory Calhoun, Lois Maxwell, Dorothy Peterson, Charles Kemper, Conrad Janis, Penny Edwards, Jean Porter, Harry Davenport, Nella Walker, Winifred Harris, Moroni Olsen, Frank Conroy, Kathryn Card, Douglas Kennedy, Barbara Brown, Tom Fadden, Jane Hamilton, William B. Davidson.* Dir.: Peter Godfrey. Pro.: Alex Gottlieb. (Warners.) Rel.: Dec. 13.

Three Weird Sisters. Not always credible story of three Welsh old maids (*Nancy Price, Mary Clare, Mary Merrall*) who in order to try and carry out their promise to restore some local houses, ruined by a cave-in of their father's worked-out coal-mine, make various attempts to murder their business-like half-brother (*Raymond Lovell*) so they can get his money. From the novel by Charlotte Armstrong. Rest of cast : *Nova Pilbeam, Anthony Hulme, Elwyn Brook-Jones, Edward Rigby, Hugh Griffith, Marie Ault, David Davies, Hugh Pryse, Lloyd Pearson, Bartlett Mullins, Doreen Richards, Frank Crawshaw, Frank Dunlop, Elizabeth Maude, Belinda Marshall, D. J. Tawe-Jones, Wilfred Boyle, Lionel Gadsden, John Humphreys, Ursula Granville, Ethel Beal, Dora Levis, Helen Lee, Elizabeth Allen.* Dir.: Dan Birt. Pro.: Louis H. Jackson. (British National.) Rel.: July 12.

Too Many Winners. Michael Shayne (*Hugh Beaumont*) beats some race-course racketeers. Rest of cast : *Trudy Marshall, Ralph Dunn, Claire Carleton, Charles Mitchell, John Hamilton, Grandon Rhodes, Ben Welden, Byron Foulger, Jean Andrew, George Meader, Frank Hagney, Maurice B. Mozelle.* Dir.: William Beaudine. Pro.: John Sutherland. (Pathe.) Rel.: Aug. 2.

To The Ends of the Earth. Dick Powell, still tough but not quite as tough as recently, as U.S. agent, tracks some dope smugglers half-way round the world. Factual treatment doesn't make the story more credible, though it it quite entertaining. Rest of cast : *Signe Hasso, Maylia, Ludwig Donath, Vladimir Sokoloff, Edgar Barrier, John Hoyt, Marcel Journet, Luis Van Rooten, Fritz Leiber, Vernon Steele, Peter Virgo, Lou Krugman, Eddie Lee, Ivan .Triesault, Leon Lenoir, Peter Chong, George Volk, Robert Malcolm, Commissioner Harry J. Anslinger.* Dir.: Robert Stevenson. Pro.: Sidney Buchman. (Columbia.) Rel.: Sept.

Trailing Danger. Western. Cast : *Johnny Mack Brown, Raymond Hatton, Peggy Wynne, Marshall Reed, Patrick Desmond, Steve Darrell, Edwin Parker, Bonnie Jean Hartley, Ernie Adams, Bud Osborne, Cactus Mack, Kansas Moehring, Gary Garrett, Dee Cooper.* Dir.: Lambert Hillyer. Pro.: Barney A. Sarecky. (Pathe.) Rel.: Oct. 4.

Trapped By Boston Blackie. *Chester* (Boston) *Morris* involved in a pearl robbery. Rest of cast : *June Vincent, Richard Lane, Patricia White, Edward Norris, George H. Stone, Frank Sully, Fay Daker, William Forrest.* Dir.: Seymour Friedman. Pro.: Rudolph C. Flothon. (Columbia.) Rel.: Oct. 25.

Tycoon. Technicolored melodrama set in South America. *John Wayne* as railroad engineer carrying the line through against great odds and winning *Laraine Day,* his boss's daughter, in the same way. Spectacular climax. Rest of cast : *Sir Cedric Hardwicke, Judith Anderson, James Gleason, Grant Withers, Anthony Quinn, Paul Fix.* Dir.: Richard Wallace. Pro.: Stephen Ames. (R.K.O. Radio.) Rel.: Not fixed.

U Unconquered. Typical 2½-hour Cecil B. De Mille Technicolored historical drama ; large, sprawling and with every tried and trusted ingredient of popular movie. The date is 1763 and the place is Fort Pitt, a lonely outpost of the edge of the Red Indian country which is today the great city of Pittsburgh. It is the story of the last great uprising of the Indian

John Wayne (extreme left) in TYCOON— R.K.O. Radio.

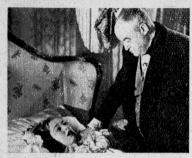

Eleanor Parker and Sydney Greenstreet in THE WOMAN IN WHITE—Warner.

tribes ; more particularly is it the story of Scout *Gary Cooper*, white renegade *Howard Da Silva* and lovely little bond slave *Paulette Goddard*. Bloody, exciting, romantic. Rest of cast : *Cecil Kellaway, Ward Bond, Virginia Campbell, Katherine de Mille, Mike Mazurki, Boris Karloff, Robert Warwick, Marc Lawrence, Richard Gaines, Alan Napier, Gavin Muir, Victor Varconi, Henry Wilcoxon, John Mylong, Oliver Thorndike, Virginia Grey, Nan Sunderland, C. Aubrey Smith*. Dir. and Pro. : De Mille. (Paramount.) Rel. : Aug. 30.

Uneasy Terms. Typical thick-ear private detection melodrama which introduces to the screen for the first time the famous Peter Cheyney character, Slim Callaghan (played by *Michael Rennie*). Mr. Callaghan's methods are unconventional, unconvincing—and surprisingly effective ! Rest of cast : *Moira Lister, Faith Brook, Joy Shelton, Patricia Goddard, Barry Jones, Marie Ney, Paul Carpenter, Nigel Patrick, Sydney Tafler, J. H. Roberts, Joan Carol, Mary Horn, John Robinson, Tony Quinn, George Street, John England, Etienne Bonichon, Harry Brooks, Chick Rolfe, Roy Russell, Lionel Newbold, Mark Stone, Julien Henry, Gordon Plunkett, Kathleen Heath, George Rigby, Raphael Norman, William Forbes, Robert Moore, Clifford Buckton, William Bridger, Delia Digby, Doreen English, Margaret Allworthy, Alec Bernard*. Dir. : Vernon Sewell. Pro. : Louis H. Jackson. (British National.) Rel. : July 5.

The Unfinished Dance. Lavish, Technicolored and generally very expensive re-make of the French ballet film " La Mort du Cygne." It is excellent entertainment even if it has nothing of the simple, almost naive charm of the original. The story concerns a child (*Margaret O'Brien*) who is in love with the premier ballerina (*Cyd Charisse*) of her ballet school. When a famous visitor (*Karin Booth*) comes to take the leads from this idol the little girl attempts a stage black-out to ruin her performance—but pulls the wrong lever and precipitates the dancer through the stage trap door into the life of a semi-invalid. Rest of cast : *Danny Thomas, Esther Dale, Thurston Hall, Harry Hayden, Mary Eleanor Donahue, Connie Cornell, Ruth Brady, Charles Bradstreet, Ann Codee, Gregory Gay*. Dir. : Henry Koster. Pro. : Joe Pasternak. (Metro-Goldwyn-Mayer.) Rel. : Aug. 9.

The Unsuspected. Excellent if somewhat over-complicated murder mystery with *Claude Rains* as star of a radio murder series who takes his talents into real life when he finds out the girl he imagined dead, and on whose fortune he is living, is very much alive and kicking. Rest of cast : *Joan Caulfield, Audrey Totter, Constance Bennett, Hurd Hatfield, Michael North, Fred Clark, Harry Lewis, Jack Lambert, Roy Walker, Nana Bryant, Walter Baldwin*. Dir. : Michael Curtiz. Pro. : Charles Hoffman. (Warner.) Rel. : Sept. 20.

V Violence. *Nancy Coleman, Michael O'Shea* and the F.B.I. break up an American Fascist organisation. Rest of cast : *Emory Parnell, Sheldon Leonard, Peter Whitney, Richard Irving, Frank Reicher, Pierre Watkin, John Hamilton, Billy Green, Drew Demerest, Carol Donne, Jimmy Clark, William Ruhl, Dick Rich, Frank Cady, Harry Depp, Helen Servis, Mary Donovan, Cay Forester*. Dir. : Jack Bernhard. Pro. :

Jack Bernhard and Bernhard Brandt. (Pathe.) Rel. : Sept. 6.

W The Weaker Sex. Film based on the Esther McCracken play, " No Medals " (formerly titled **No Medals for Martha, The Housewives Story**, etc.). It was written in praise of the way women carried on at home during the war ; their worries, sorrows and triumphs. Cast : *Ursula Jeans, Cecil Parker, Joan Hopkins, Derek Bond, Lana Morris, John Stone, Thora Hird, Digby Wolfe, Marion Spencer*. Dir. : Roy Baker. Pro. : Paul Soskin. (Two Cities.) Rel. : Oct. 11.

West of Pecos. Western with *Robert Mitchum* as cowboy Pecos Smith. Rest of cast : *Barbara Hale, Richard Martin, Thurston Hall, Rita Corday, Russell Hopton, Bill Williams, Bruce Edwards, Harry Woods, Perc Launders, Bryant Washburn, Philip Morris, Martin Garralaga*. Dir. : Edward Killy. Pro. : Herman Schlom. (R.K.O. Radio.) Rel. : Sept. 20.

When A Girl's Beautiful. Romance of a model, *Adele Jergens*. Rest of cast : *Marc Platt, Patricia White, Stephen Dunne, Steven Geray, Mona Barrie, Jack Leonard, Paul Harvey, Lela Bliss, Nancy Saunders, Doris Houck, Amelita Ward, Peggy Call, Vera Stokes, Thomas Louden*. Dir. : Frank McDonald. (Columbia.) Rel. : Sept. 27.

Whispering Smith. Technicolored, outdoor 1890 melodrama with two-gun detective Whispering Smith (*Alan Ladd*) up against his former friend, now outlaw (*Robert Preston*), whose wife—to complicate matters—is loved by *Ladd*. Rest of cast : *Brenda Marshall, Donald Crisp, William Demarest, Fay Holden, Frank Faylen, John Eldredge, J. Farrell MacDonald, Don Barclay, Murvyn Vye, Robert Wood, Robert Kortman, Will Wright*. Dir. : Leslie Fenton. Pro. : Paramount Rel. : Not fixed—likely to be Dec.

The Winslow Boy. Screen adaptation of the Terence Rattigan play based on a true incident of Naval history. The Winslow boy is accused of theft, his father fights the charge right to the House of Lords and eventually clears the lad. Cast : *Robert Donat, Margaret Leighton, Sir Cedric Hardwicke, Marie Lohr, Neil North, Jack Watling, Frank Lawton, Nicholas Hannen, Basil Radford, Kathleen Harrison, Evelyn Roberts, Walter Fitzgerald, Francis L. Sullivan, Wilfred Hyde White, Mona Washbourne, Billy Shine, Anthony Bird, Barry Briggs, Cecil Bevan, Wilfred Caithness, Lambert Ensom, Hugh Dempster, Archibald Batty, Philip Ray, W. A. Kelley, Edward Lexy, Gordon McLeod, George Bishop, P. Kynaston Reeves, Charles Groves, Ian Colin, Ivan Samson, Ernest Thesiger, Dandy Nicholls, Vera Cook, Sir Lewis Casson, Stanley Holloway, Cyril Ritchard, Jane Gill Davies, Frank Tickle, Honor Blake, Margaret Withers, Noel Howlett, Aubrey Mallalieu, Mary Hinton, Nicholas Hawtrey, Beatrice Marsden, Hilary Pritchard*. Dir. : Anthony Asquith. Pro. : Anatole de Grunwald. (International Screen Plays.) Rel. : Nov. 8.

Winter Meeting. First *Bette Davis* film in three years, this is a very much dialogue-weighted romance between a poetess and a naval officer who after a lot of argument decides that his future happiness lies in the priesthood rather than Miss Davis. Rest of cast : *Janis Paige, James Davis, John Hoyt, Florence Bates, Walter Baldwin, Ransom Sherman*. Dir. : Bretaigne Windust. Pro. : Henry Blanke. (Warner.) Rel. : Dec. 20.

The Wistful Widow. *Bud Abbott* and *Lou Costello* get mixed up in a very wild and extremely woolly West, ably assisted by wistful widow *Marjorie Main*. A typical A. and C. slapstick romp. Rest of cast : *George Cleveland, Gordon Jones, William Ching, Peter Thompson, Olin Howlin, Bill Clauson, Pamela Wells, Jimmie Bates, Paul Dunn, Diane Florentine, Rex Lease, Glenn Strange, Edmund Cobb, Wade Crosby, Dewey Robinson, Murray Leonard*. Dir. : Charles T. Barton. Pro. : Robert Arthur. (Universal-International.) Rel. : Nov. 15.

Woman Hater. Stewart Granger in his first comedy plays a woman-hating man who, like all men in the end, finds his hate wearing thin when confronted by the luscious curves and clever scheming of *Edwige Feuillere*. Rest of cast : *Jeanne de Casalis, Ronald Squire, David Hutcheson, Mary Jerrold, W. A. Kelly, Georgina Cookson, Henry Edwards, Stewart Rome, H. G. Stoker, Valentine Dyall, Richard Hearne, Cyril Ritchard, Michael Medwin, John Stevens, Anne Holland, Vida Hope, Graham Moffat, Dino Galvani, Vernon Greeves, Rosemary Treston, Diana Chandler, Margaret Thorburn, Barbara Gurnhill, Diana Hope, Doreen Lawrence, Jeremy Annett, Peter Cotten, Miles Malleson*. Dir. : Terence Young. Pro. : William Sistrom. (Two Cities.) Rel. : Nov. 15.

The Woman in White. Excellent screen version of the famous 1850 mystery story written by Wilkie Collins. Cast : *Alexis Smith, Eleanor Parker, Sydney Greenstreet, Gig Young, Agnes Moorehead, John Abbott, John Emery, Curt Bois, Emma Dunn, Matthew Boulton, Anita Sharp-Bolster, Clifford Brooke, Barry Bernard*. Dir. : Peter Godfrey. Pro. : Henry Blanke. (Warner.) Rel : Aug. 30.

The World and His Wife. (" State of The Union " in America). Based on the play of the latter title, this is a typical Frank Capra production (he both directed and produced it). It concerns an honest business man who gets mixed up with crooked politicians when he is persuaded to run for President, his unhappy suppression of conscience and final outburst over the adio, when he tells America just what kind of dishonest wretches many of her political leaders are and the chicanery with which they get into power. Sentimental, warm, noisy, patriotic and with a basis of sound common sense. And grand screen entertainment, too A wonderful performance by *Spencer Tracy*, a better-than-average one from *Katharine Hepburn* as his wife and a surprising one from *Angela Lansbury* as *Tracy's* newspaper-owning girl-friend. Good work, too, from *Adolphe Menjou* and *Van Johnson*. Rest of cast : *Lewis Stone, Howard Smith, Charles Dingle, Maidel Turner, Raymond Walburn, Margaret Hamilton, Art Baker, Pierre Watkin, Florence Auer, Irving Bacon, Charles Lane, Patti Brady, George Nokes, Carl " Alfalfa " Switzer, Tom Fadden, Tom Pedi*. Dir. and Pro. : Frank Capra. (Liberty-M.-G.-M.) Rel. : Oct. 4.

The Wreck of the Hesperus. Action-filled period maritime drama. Cast : *Willard Parker, Edgar Buchanan, Patricia White, Holmes Herbert, Wilton Graff, Boyd Davis, Jeff Corey, Paul Campbell, Paul E. Burns, Trevor Bardette, Herbert Heywood*. Dir. : John Hoffman Pro. : Wallace MacDonald. (Columbia.) Rel. : Nov. 22.

Y You Were Meant For Me. Pleasing, modest little musical set in the 1920's, with band leader *Dan Dailey* marrying *Jeanne Crain* and going through the slump before finding fame. Oscar Levant providing some delightful, dry humour. Rest of cast : *Barbara Lawrence Selena Royle, Percy Kilbride, Herbert Anderson*. Dir. : Lloyd Bacon. Pro. : Fred Kohlmar. (20th Century-Fox.) Rel. : Aug. 23.

Ballerina Karin Booth and Margaret O'Brien in THE UNFINISHED DANCE—Metro-Goldwyn-Mayer.

1947 RELEASES

FOOTNOTE

Last year I introduced for the first time, as a kind of Footnote (its actual title) to the list of the year's releases an appendix, a separate section devoted to the releases of the previous year (1946, that is) which had escaped inclusion in the 1946-47 Film Review.

At this point maybe I had better once more explain—as I explain every year—that such omissions are almost inevitable in view of the very natural and correct decision of the publisher that in order that FILM REVIEW shall be completely topical it must each year be on sale before that particular year has actually ended ; a decision which means that the book must go to the printers in the autumn, and though every effort is made at the last possible moment to complete the list of the year's releases between this September press date and the end of the year, it always happens —the movie business being what it is—that a few unexpected films come along out of the blue and throw one's forecast out of gear.

Kieron Moore—as Salvatore, the murder-minded major domo—tries to quieten the serving girl (Maria Fimiani), but too late. The mistress of the House (Margaret Johnston with lamp) has heard everything—A MAN ABOUT THE HOUSE—British Lion.

A Likely Story. Neat if never gaudy little comedy about a discharged soldier who by a misunderstanding thinks he only has two weeks to live. Cast : *Barbara Hale, Bill Williams, Sam Levene, Lanny Rees, Dan Tobin, Nestor Paiva, Max Willenz, Henry Kuley, Robin Raymond, Mary Young.* Dir. : H. C. Potter. Pro. : Richard H. Berger. (R.K.O. Radio.) Rel. : Oct. 7, 1947.

A Man About the House. Screen adaptation of the Francis Brett Young novel, dramatised into a successful play by John Perry, about two spinsters from North Bromwich who inherit a lovely Italian villa. One falls for the charms of the ambitious Italian major domo, who marries her and nearly murders her in his greed to get his hand on the land which he covets so much. *Margaret Johnston* is the unhappy, repressed woman ; *Dulcie Gray* plays her sister and *Kieron Moore* makes an impressive screen debut as the Italian. Rest of cast : *Guy Middleton, Felix Aylmer, Lilian Braithwaite, Jone Salinas, Maria Fimiani, Fulvia de Priamo, Nicola Esposito, Reginald Purdell, Wilfred Caithness.* Dir. : Leslie Arliss. Pro. : Edward Black. (British Lion.) Rel. : Nov. 4, 1947.

Blondie in the Dough. When Dagwood irritates his boss's potential client on the golf course wife Blondie comes to the rescue. Cast : *Penny Singleton, Arthur Lake, Larry Simms, Marjorie Kent, Jerome Cowan, Hugh Herbert, Clarence Kolb, Danny Mummert, William Forrest, Eddie Acuff, Norman Phillips, Kernan Cripps.* (Columbia.) Rel. : Oct. 28, 1947.

Crimson Key. Detective Kent Taylor is engaged by a doctor's wife to solve the mystery of her husband's worries. Rest of cast : *Doris Dowling, Dennis Hoey, Louise Currie, Ivan Triesault, Arthur Space, Vera Marshe, Edwin Rand, Bernadene Hayes, Victoria Horne, Doug Evans, Ann Doran, Victor Sen Yung, Chester Clute, Ralf Harolde, Milton Parsons, Jimmy Magill, Marietta Canty, Stanley Mann.* Dir. : Eugene Forde. Pro. : Sol M. Wurtzel. (20th Century-Fox.) Rel. : Nov. 3, 1947.

Desperate. Medium paced but generally exciting gangster piece. Cast : *Steve Brodie, Audrey Long, Raymond Burr, Douglas Fowley, William Challee, Jason Robards, Freddie Steele, Lee Fredericks, Paul E. Burns, Ilka Gruning.* Dir. : Anthony Mann. Pro. : Michel Kraike. (R.K.O. Radio.) Rel. : Oct. 21, 1947.

The Devil Thumbs a Ride. *Lawrence Tierney* is wanted for murder, persuades a commercial traveller to give him a lift, then persuades him to pick up two girl hitch-hikers—then starts murdering again. Rest of cast : *Ted North,*

Nan Leslie, Betty Lawford, Andrew Tombes, Harry Shannon, Glenn Vernon, Marian Carr, William Gould, Josephine Whittell, Phil Warren, Robert Malcolm. Dir. : Felix Feist. Pro. : Herman Schlom. (R.K.O. Radio.) Rel. : Dec. 15, 1947.

Dick Tracy v. Cueball. Tracy is called in to solve the mystery of the strangled jewel importer and the missing diamonds. Cast : *Morgan Conway, Anne Jeffreys, Lyle Latell, Rita Corday, Ian Keith, Dick Wesel, Douglas Walton, Esther Howard, Joseph Crehan, Byron Foulger, Jimmy Crane, Milton Parsons, Skelton Knaggs.* Dir. : Gordon M. Douglas. Pro. : Herbert Schlom. (R.K.O. Radio.) Rel. : Nov. 18, 1947.

Fame is the Spur. Long, slow, thoughtful but occasionally dull, imaginative biography of a left-wing politician who sells out everything and everyone, even including his own wife, in his ambitious search for political power. From the well-known Howard Spring novel of the same title. Cast : *Michael Redgrave (as the politician), Rosamund John, Hugh Burden, Bernard Miles, Carla Lehmann, Sir Seymour Hicks, David Tomlinson, Marjorie Fielding, Charles Wood, Milton Rosmer, Wylie Watson, Anthony Wager, Brian Weske, Gerald Fox, Jean Shepheard, Guy Verney, Percy Walsh.* Dir. : Roy Boulting. Pro. : John Boulting. (Two Cities.) Rel. : Nov. 4, 1947.

Politician Hamer Redshaw (Michael Redgrave) sees his friend (Hugh Burden) arrested for the riot that he knows he started himself. A scene from the Two Cities film FAME IS THE SPUR.

High Conquest. The eternal triangle on the slopes of the Matterhorn ; passions against a background of coldly indifferent peaks. Cast : *Anna Lee, Gilbert Roland, Warren Douglas, Beulah Bondi, C. Aubrey Smith, John Qualen, Helene Thimig, Alan Napier, Eric Feldary, Mickey Kuhn, Louis Mercier, Richard Flato.* Dir. and Pro. : Irving Allen. (Pathe.) Rel. : Nov. 25, 1947.

Key Witness. Slow, unexciting murder melo about a man trying to escape from a crime he hasn't committed. Cast : *John Beal, Trudy Marshall, Jimmy Lloyd, Helen Mowery, Wilton Graff, Barbara Reed, Charles Trowbridge, Harry Hayden, William Newell, Selmer Jackson, Robert Williams.* Dir. : D. Ross Lederman. Pro. : Rudolph Flothow. (Columbia.) Rel. : Nov. 11, 1947.

Mark of the Claw. Dick Tracy (*Ralph Byrd*) thriller. Rest of cast : *Jimmy Conlin, Jack Lambert, Ian Keith, Kay Christopher, Lyle Latell, Bernadene Hayes, William B. Davidson, Tony Barrett, Richard Powers.* Dir. : John Rawlins. Pro. : Herbert Schlom. (R.K.O. Radio.) Rel. : Oct. 28, 1947.

San Quentin. *Lawrence Tierney* as reformed convict tracking down a bank robber in order to vindicate his Prisoners' Welfare League

Rest of cast : *Barton MacLane, Marian Carr, Harry Shannon, Carol Forman, Richard Powers, Joe Devlin, Tony Barrett, Lee Bonnell, Robert Clarke.* Dir. : Gordon M. Douglas. Pro. : Martin Mooney. (R.K.O. Radio.) Rel. : Dec. 1, 1947.

The Silver Darlings. Somewhat confused but occasionally interesting little British film which sets out rather over ambitiously to tell the story of the Scots herring fleet. Cast : *Norman Williams, Christopher Capon, Murdo Morrison, Helen Shingler, Carl Bernard, Stanley Jay, Harry Fine, Phyllis Morris, Clifford Evans, Iris Vandeleur, Jean Shepherd, Norman Shelley, Simon Lack, Bennett O'Loghlin, Carole Lesley, Josephine Stuart, Jack Faint, Wilfred Caithness, Michael Martin Harvey, Anne Allan, Phema Clyne, Hugh Griffith, Peter Illing, Roddy Hughes, Hamilton Deane, Ken Warrington.* Dir. : Clarence Elder. Pro. : Karl Grune. (Pathe.) Rel. : Dec. 8, 1947.

They Won't Believe Me. Intelligent, thoughtful movie about a no-good who marries mainly for money and can never let love get first place in his heart. Ironically he is caught and tried for the one dirty thing he hasn't done—the murder of his wife. *Robert Young* is excellent as the waster, *Rita Johnson* as his unfortunate wife, *Jane Greer* and *Susan Hayward* are other women in his life. Rest of cast : *Tom Powers, George Tyne, Don Beddoe, Frank Ferguson, Harry Harvey.* Dir. : Irving Pichel. Pro. : Joan Harrison. (R.K.O. Radio.) Rel. : Dec. 1, 1947.

Wake Up and Dream. A flimsy little whimsy in colour about a little girl who goes sailing over land and ocean in a neighbour's home-made boat and discovers her brother, who everyone thinks has been lost at sea. Treatment is a little heavy-handed. Cast : *John Payne, June Haver, Charlotte Greenwood, Connie Marshall, John Ireland, Clem Bevans, Charles Russell, Lee Patrick, Charles D. Brown, Irving Bacon.* Dir. : Lloyd Bacon. Pro. : Walter Morosco. (20th Century-Fox.) Rel. : Nov. 4, 1947.

Will Tomorrow Ever Come ? A small-time accountant buys a horse, meets a girl. He marries the girl, races the colt. Gambles away his money and has to start all over again as a reformed character. Cast : *Don Ameche, Catherine McLeod, Roscoe Karns, Gregory Marshall, Dorothy Adams, Frankie Darro, John Riagely, Kitty Irish, Joe Frisco, Hampton J. Scott, John Miljan, William B. Davidson, Joe Hernandez.* Dir. and Pro. : Frank Borzage. (British Lion-Republic.) Rel. : Dec. 1, 1947.

Playboy Robert Young, determined to at last cut the cash-knot which binds him to his long suffering wife (Rita Johnson-not in the picture) plans to run away with gold-digger Susan Hayward—R.K.O. Radio's THEY WON'T BELIEVE ME.

EASILY the most obvious and outstanding point that arises in any, even cursory, examination of the various foreign films that have been shown in this country during the year is the emergence into the sun of the Italian film. It is the Italian moviemakers who have stolen top honours, held so long before the war by the French—today still below their best standard and though occasionally brilliant quite as often dull—and from whom are now coming the most completely satisfying movies of this period.

Films like *Four Steps in the Clouds*, *Shoe Shine* and *Vivere in Pace* have all shown a common warmth, a deep human understanding and a fine sympathetic humour which make them works of considerable artistic worth. These films have pulsed with real life and been about real people ; here, in fact, was richness. Yet all these films, often technically indifferent, were made on minor budgets. They triumphed because they had heart in them. Yes, 1948 was definitely Italy's year, I think.

Of the French movies *Farrabique* (with its observant and technically novel recital of the four seasons and their effect on a small French farm) was easily the most interesting, probably the most brilliant. *La Belle et La Bete*, Jean Cocteau's bizarre version of the old fairy story was the most curious, *Bataille du Rail* (the work of the French

(*Left*) ALFRED ADAM played a sex maniac in the deep-running LA FERME DU PENDU, which concerned one man's lust for the land and the way it affects his family. Adam played one of the man's two brothers and is seen here with CLAUDINE DUPUIS in one of the film's "outspoken" seduction scenes. The censor held up the picture ; it was finally shown on a London A licence.

(*Right*) LE CORBEAU, a story about a poison pen letter writer, was interesting in that it was one of the few French films we have seen that was made during the German occupation. It was grim, slightly unpleasant, but well made and extremely ably acted. Here is PIERRE FRESNAY, a doctor and a suspect, with sultry patient GINETTE LECLERC, another suspect.

A little flirtation between JACQUES BOREL and JEANNE MARKEN in Jean Renoir's PARTIE DE CAMPAGNE, a short film based on a Guy de Maupassant short story.

Half documentary, half fiction, but acted entirely by an amateur cast of French Railway Resisters, BATAILLE DU RAIL (awarded the 1946 Cannes Festival Grand Prix International Award) was a breathlessly exciting recital of the way the French railway workers sabotaged the German war plans, sometimes paying for their bravery with their lives. Here the local Maquis wait for the train carrying German reinforcements to the Normandy front, determined that the train shall never get there.

Railwaymen's resistance movement) the most exciting, Jean-Paul Sartre's (the " Existentialist ") *Les Jeux Sont Faits* the most oddly depressing, and *L'Homme au Chapeau Rond* the most pathetic in that it marked the tragic end of the career of that great French actor, Raimu.

Films from countries other than Italy and France have been few and far between. Most interesting was the first post-war German film : the brilliant, absorbing anti-Nazi picture *The Murderers Are Amongst Us*. This showed the German movie-makers have lost none of the cunning that once made their productions lead the world ; nor have they lost any of their typically Germanic gloom. But *The Murderers* was a tremendously well worth-while film which no student of the contemporary cinema should have missed.

The year also saw the advent of the first Argentine movie to be shown here, *Spanish Serenade*—a long, polished, well acted and slightly boring production. The list is completed by a naive, unusual, religious Swedish film, *The Road to Heaven*.

Still to be seen, as I write, are several films due for late 1948 showing and promised as something outstanding.

They include *Le Diable Au Corps*, with Micheline Presle and Gerard Philipe ; the international prize film *Monsieur Vincent*, with Pierre Fresnay ; *Au Revenant* with Louis Jouvet and Gaby Morlay; the Italian *Piaser*, directed by Roberto Rosselini, the man who made *Open City* ; *Antoine et Antoinette* (which took first prize at the Cannes Festival) and an Italian film of *Rigoletto* starring Tito Gobbi.

JEAN MARAIS, as the beast, carries fainting beauty JOSETTE DAY along a corridor lit with flambeaux held by disembodied arms, a scene from Jean Cocteau's bizarre adaptation of the old fairy story, LA BELLE ET LA BETE.

In the last film he made before he died of cancer, L'HOMME AU CHAPEAU ROND, RAIMU played tragedy, taking the role of a man whose wife has deceived him and who is determined to take revenge on the man, his friend, who has caused him his unhappiness.

Long ago it was proved that the camera can lie, as it does here. Double-exposure trick photography makes you think that LOUIS JOUVET is threatening himself in this scene from MONSIEUR ALIBI, a comedy in which he played the role of an arch-crook and his innocent, poor-but-honest double.

SHOE SHINE was an Italian film about juvenile delinquency; a tragic story of two small boys whose dabble in the black market leads to a reformatory term and, eventually, to sudden death. Here the boys are being interviewed in the police station.

In QUAI DES ORFEVRES, a French whodunnit, LOUIS JOUVET gave a delightfully whimsical performance as a detective who is also very much of a human being and family man. Here he is with the curvacious SUZY DELAIR (also inset).

FOREIGN FILMS OF 1948

Antoine et Antoinette. Winning film at the 1947 Cannes Film Festival. A story of a printer and his young wife; they dream of fortune and good things and eventually win a lottery. But then they find they have lost their ticket. . . . Background is the Paris of the working classes. Grand little comedy. Cast *Roger Pigaut, Claire Maffei, Annette Poivre, Noel Roquevert, Jacques Meyran, Gaston Modit.* Dir.: Jacques Becker. Pro.: C. F. Tavano. (Siritzky.) First shown at Rialto in Sept. 1948.

L'Ange de la Nuit—Angel of the Dark. French film about a young sculptor who goes to war—comes back blinded. Helpless, he turns to another student for aid, falls in love with her. She, thinking her own fiancé must be dead, agrees to marriage. Then the missing boy turns up and with him brings the girl a tremendous problem. A slow, talkie film but one with moving passages. Beautifully acted by *Jean-Louis Barrault* as the blinded sculptor and *Michele Alfa* as the girl. Rest of cast: *Henry Vidal, Gaby Andreu, Larquey, Alice Tissot, Yves Furet, Claire Jordan, Cynette Quero.* Dir.: Berthomieu. Pro.: Raymond Borderei. First shown at Academy in Jan. 1948.

Au Petit Bonheur. One of the most completely crazy comedies ever to come from the French studios; based on the old plot of the neglected wife who makes her husband fall in love with her by first making him jealous. Cast: *Danielle Darrieux, Francois Perier, Andre Luguet, Paulette Dubost, Henri Cremieux, Pasquali.* Dir: Marcel L'Herbier. First shown at Studio One in Sept. 1947.

Bataille du Rail, is a long, factual, exciting and extremely well made pictorial account of the part that the French railwaymen played in the Underground movement during the German Occupation. Made by the men who did the job. An altogether outstanding picture; documentary in character but acted with complete sincerity and realism; richly human, intensely exciting. This film won the Grand Prix International at Cannes in 1946. Cast: *Salina Daurand, Lozach, Pauleon, Desagneaux, Clarens, Clarieux, Barnault Kronegger,* and the men of the French Railways. Dir: Rene Clement. First shown at Academy in Oct. 1947.

La Belle et la Bete. Jean Cocteau's film version of the fairy story of **The Beauty and the Beast.** Involved and confusing, with a good deal of

ENRICO IV was an Italian film based on the Pirandello play of the same title, about a madman who becomes sane but in sanity kills, so has to go back to feigning madness. Here Osvaldo Valenti admits to Luigi Pavese (left), Clara Calami, Enzo Biliotti and Lauro Gazzalo that in spite of his continued masquerade as the Emperor Henry IV he has actually been sane for some considerable time.

symbolism. Cocteau heightens the fantastic atmosphere of the story with all kinds of queer, occasionally surrealistic touches—flambeaux of human arms that turn to light the wayfarer along his path, decorative heads in the mantel that blink, gloves that smoke. A most unusual, certainly very interesting picture. *Jean Marais* as The Beast; *Josette Day* as the (blonde) Beauty who comes to love him in spite of his

PORTES DE LA NUIT was slow confusing; full of undertones, artistic, imaginative and, in fact, a collector's piece. It concerned the fantastic events of a single night in Paris; was made by Marcel Carne. Here are Nathalie Nattier and Pierre Brasseur.

awesome appearance and strange habits. Rest of cast: *Marcel André, Mila Parely, Nane Germon, Michel Auclair.* Dir. & Pro.: Jean Cocteau. (Andre Paulve Production). First shown at Rialto in Nov. 1947.

Le Corbeau—The Crow. Brilliant French film. A quiet, sunny and peaceful little French village is suddenly stirred by the arrival of an anonymous letter. Before it has recovered another is sent, and soon the letters start to pour in. In the resultant atmosphere of suspicion and distrust each man looks to his neighbour. There is suicide and murder before the criminal is discovered and the crime avenged. *Pierre Fresnay* is excellent as the doctor against whom most of the slander is aimed; *Ginette Leclerc* as good as the crippled girl sensualist who loves him. Wonderful performances also come from many of the supporting players: *Pierre Larquey, Noel Roquevert, Bernard Lancret, Antoine Balpetre, Jean Brochard, Pierre Bertin, Louis Seigner, Robert Clermont, Gustave Gallet, Palau, Marcel Delaitre, Etienne Decroux, Albert Malbert, Ginette Leclerc, Micheline Francey, Helena Manson, Jeanne Fusier-Gir, Sylvie, Liliane Maigne.* Dir.: Henri-Georges Clouzot. First shown at Rialto in March 1948.

Le Diable au Corps. A love story which starts at the end of the 1914 Great War. Due at Studio One, London, late 1948. With *Micheline Presle, Gerard Philipe, Denis Grey, Paulau* and *Jean Debucourt.* Dir.: Louis Wipf. Pro.: Paul Graetz.

Enrico IV. Italian picture based on Pirandello play about a man who has a fall from his horse and goes mad, imagines he is the eleventh century Emperor, Henry IV. After 20 years he recovers his mind, only to commit a murder. So if he is to escape justice he is faced with the knowledge that until the end of his days he must go on pretending he is mad! An excellent play made into an interesting if somewhat static film. A wonderful performance by *Osvaldo Valenti* as the madman. Rest of cast: *Clara Calamai, Luigi Pavese, Lauro Gazzalo, Checco Rissone, Augusto Marcacci, Ori Monteverdi, Giorgio Piamonti, Enzo Biliotti, Ruby D'Alma.* Dir: Giogio Pastina. Pro.: Piero Caaserini. First shown at Academy, London, in March 1948.

Farrebique, or **The Four Seasons.** Beautiful French semi-documentary account of a year of the life on a large provincial farm in the

Ludmilla Tcherina as Karina, a very heartless ballerina in **UN REVENANT**, which stars Louis Jouvet (not seen in this scene). With her is young Francois (Francois Perier) who will satisfy her whim for an hour—or a day.

Rouergue district of Aveyron (Central France). About the family, their births and deaths; the animals, the birds and the trees. It took a year to make. The director makes a novel use of creeping shadows to denote passing time. A simple, charming film. Awarded the 1946 Nice Grand Prix de la Critique Internationale and Grand Prix du Cinema Francaise. Dir.: Georges Rouquier. Pro.: Jacqueline Jacoupy. First shown at Curzon in March 1948.

La Ferme Du Pendu. Deep, leisurely French film based on the old theme of the peasant's lust for the land. In this case it's the story of three brothers and a sister. The youngest brother yearns for a garage, the second is a sex maniac (a hobby that leads to his downfall and death) and the sister goes after the bright lights; it is left to the elder brother (superbly played by *Charles Vanel*) to slave and in the end kill himself so that their lands shall stay intact and in good heart. A fine, quiet film, as noteworthy for its acting as for its glimpses of authentic French provincial life. Rest of cast: *Alfred Adam, Guy Decomble, Arlette Merry, Lucienne Laurence, Marthe Mellot, Claudine Dupuis, Bever.* Dir.: Jean Dreville. First shown at Academy in July 1948.

The Idiot. Well made, quite excellent film based on the difficult subject of a novel of the same title by Dostoievsky. The story concerns various characters, each searching for his own personal happiness. Cast: *Gerard Phillippe, Edwige Feuillere, Marguerite Moreno, Lucien Coedel.* Dir.: Georges Lampin. Pro.: Sacha Gordine. First shown at La Continental, London.

Gerard Philipe looks through the railway carriage window at the girl (co-star Micheline Presle) he loves in this scene from **LE DIABLE AU CORPS.**

Les Jeux Sont Faits. A most interesting and somewhat "deep" film about life and after-life written by Jean Paul Sartre, originator of the strangely titled "Existentialism"; about a rich wife and a poor man who meet after they die and think they should have been born for each other. Accordingly they get 24 hours back on earth to prove that they would, in fact, live only for each other. But they fail; he cannot forget his comrades who are about to be sacrificed, she cannot tamely submit to watch her sister seduced by her husband. A quite brilliant, essentially Gallic, mixture of wistful fantasy, melancholia, poetry, imagination and deft, satirical humour. Finely acted by new star *Micheline Presle* (as the woman), *Marcel Pagliero* (as the man). Rest of cast: *Jacques Erwin, Edmond Beauchamp, Mouloudji, Howard Vernon, Renaud Mary, Jean Daurand, Fernand Fabre, Colette Ripert, Marguerite Moreno, Guy Decomble, Jim Gerald, Paul Olivier, Charles Dullin.* Dir.: Jean Delannoy. Pro.: Louis Wipf. (Films Gibe.) First shown at Studio One in March 1948.

L'Homme au Chapeau Rond. This was the last film to be made with *Raimu* before the great French actor died of cancer. A dismal little tragedy, from Dostoievsky's "The Eternal Husband," it is about a widower who seeks a grim revenge on his friend, who has betrayed him with his wife. Not a great film, but in the central, tragic role *Raimu* gives another of his many great performances. *Aime Clariond* is also quite outstanding. Rest of cast: *Helena Manson, Maud Lamy, Colette Georges, Adrienne Allain, Gisele Alcee, Villars, Lucy Valnor, Arlette Merry, Micheline Boudet, Louis Seignier, Jane Marken, Gisele Casadesus, Therese Marney.* Dir.: Pierre Billon. (Alcina, Paris.) First shown at Academy in June 1948.

In France a writer called Jean Paul Satre started something called "Existentialism," which is too involved to be described here. But it was this same "Existentialism" which formed the theme of the film **LES JEUX SONT FAITS.** Here Micheline Presle and Marcel Pagliero, back on earth for a second chance, listen to a wandering beggar play a flute.

Les Portes de la Nuit—Portals of the Night. A collector's piece if ever there was one; slow, confusing, full of undertones and hints of deeper meanings; yet also imaginative, artistic. Only from the French could come these flashes of completely unembarrassed poetry or sudden moments of bitter irony; only from the French could come those realistic earthy characters; those dirty, everyday backgrounds, the streets of Paris, badly lit, shadowy, cobbled; with pools of stagnant water. The story of the events of one single night and how they affect the lives of a bunch of characters. Cast: *Malou, Diego, Georges, Monsieur Senechal, Raymond Lecuyer, Guy, Monsieur Quinquina, Le Clochard, Claire Lecuyer, Madame Quinquina, Cri-Cri, Etiennette.* Dir. & Pro.: Marcel Carne. First shown at Rialto in Sept. 1947.

Lunegarde. Somewhat confusing little French regeneration drama made in 1945 and showing evidence of somewhat sketchy production. Story tells of the re-uniting of misunderstood mother and her searching daughter. Cast: *Gaby Morlay, Jean Tissier, Giselle Pascal.* Dir.: R. Montis. First shown at Studio One in Jan. 1948.

Monsieur Alibi—Copie Conforme. Deft typically ironic little French comedy about a man who becomes the official, paid alibi of his double, a big-time crook. In the end he comes out of the adventure with his boss's identity, fortune and girl-friend (shapely luscious *Suzy Delair*)! *Louis Jouvet* plays the crook and his alibi. First shown at Academy in Dec. 1947.

Monsieur Vincent. International prize winning French film starring *Pierre Fresnay.* Due at Curzon, London, late in 1948. No other details to hand at press time.

The Murderers are Amongst Us. First post-war German film to be shown in Britain. Typical example of Germanic filmcraft; heavy, sombre, with plenty of shadows and a certain amount of symbolism. But most interesting and certainly well made and quite brilliantly acted. Story is about an ex-Army medical officer who was nearly driven insane by the cruelty he witnesses; eventually catches up with the superior officer responsible and

L'ANGE DE LA NUIT was a story of self sacrifice; the angel (Michele Alfa) devoting herself to war-blinded artist Jean-Louis Barrault when she thinks her lover has been killed at the front. The climax of the film occurs when the lover turns up and the angel has to make her big decision.

Maurice Chevalier returned to the screen after a nine years' absence in order to play the film director (1900 vintage) in Rene Clair's delightful LE SILENCE EST D'OR, which the latter wrote, directed and produced, and with which he won the Grand Prize at the 1947 Brussels Film Festival. With Chevalier is newcomer Marcelle Derrien.

finds him now a good father and a benevolent boss. Faced with his misdeeds he shouts, "I am not guilty, I am not guilty," as the German Nation has shouted after every war. Excellent, intelligent propaganda. Cast : *Hildegard Knef, Ernst Fischer, Arno Paulsen, Erna Sellmer, Robert Forsch, Albert Johann.* Dir.: Wolfgang Staudte. Pro.: Herbert Uhlich. First shown at Academy in April 1948.

La Nuit Fantastique—Fantastic Night. A somewhat surrealistic little comedy about a man (*Fernand Gravet*) who keeps dreaming of a girl (*Micheline Presle*) and then one day wakes to find her just disappearing into a cafe. He follows her : into the cafe, her life and a most strange and fantastic adventure. Rest of cast : *Saturnin Fabre, Bernard Blier, Charles Grandval.* Dir. & Pro.: Marcel L'Herbier. First shown at Studio One in Jan. 1948.

Paisa. Italian film in six separate episodes ; all concerning the Americans in Italy. One episode is about a negro soldier who is horrified at the poverty he discovers in tracking down his stolen shoes, another is about the tragic discovery of a soldier that the girl he met and loved six months ago is the prostitute who takes him home now, another is a touching cameo in a monastery, and so on. Dir.: Roberto Rossellini. Pro.: Rod. E. Geiger. First shown at Academy late in 1948.

Partie de Campagne. From the Guy de Maupassant short story "A Country Excursion" this is an account of a young girl who in 1860 went into the Parisian country for a day, met a man and was seduced. A gay little piece with only the ending, when seducer and seduced meet again by chance many years later, dipping into more tragic vein. Cast : *Sylvia Bataille, Georges Saint-Saens, Jeanne Marken, Gabriello, Jacques Borel, Paul Temps, Gabrielle Fontan, Jean Renoir, Marguerite Renoir.* Dir.: Jean Renoir. Pro.: Brunius. First shown at Academy in Oct. 1947.

One of the most brilliant French films of the year was FARREBIQUE, which followed the procession of the four seasons on a small, provincial French farm and how the passing of the twelve months affects its inhabitants. Here the grandfather sits by the fire.

Quai des Orfevres. A straightforward mystery story about the murder of a humpbacked sexual pervert, the sorting of suspects by patient, very human detective *Louis Jouvet* and the solution of the crime. A story made outstanding by the brilliant treatment of director Henry-Georges Clouzot, who makes every one of his characters intensely real and his backgrounds casually factual ; who manages to keep up the excitement of the story without ever letting you more than wildly guess what will happen next. An adult picture : and a very good one. Rest of cast : *Bernard Blier* (as the jealous husband), *Simone Renart* (his flighty but well-meaning, very ambitious wife), *Suzy Delair* (the very understanding and self-sacrificing Other Woman), *Charles Dullin.* Dir.: Henry-Georges Clouzot. First shown at Rialto in Jan. 1948.

Quattro Passi Fra Le Nuvole. Four Steps in the Clouds—Brilliant Italian film about a commercial traveller in confectionery, who gets turned off a train because he's forgotten his season ticket—and so gets thrown into a charming two-day adventure in which a girl who is going to have an illegitimate child persuades him to pose as her husband, so that her strict country family won't turn her out when she returns to them. A simple tale, made into classic movie by the warmth, deep understanding and acute observation of human nature displayed throughout the story. And wonderful acting performances from a cast headed by *Gino Cervi* and *Adriana Benetti* and including : *Guiditta Rissone, Carlo Romano, Guido Celano, Margherita Seglin, Aldo Silvani, Mario Siletti, Oreste Bilancia, Guido Bocci, Arturo Bragaglia, Anna Carena, Pina Callini, Armando Migliari, Luciano Manari, Giacinto Molteni.* Dir.: Alessandro Blasetti. Pro.: Giuseppe Amato. First shown at Curzon in May 1948.

Rigoletto. New Italian version of the famous opera with *Tito Gobbi* heading a famous operatic cast which includes *Maria Fillipeschi, Lina Pagliughi, Guilio Neri, Marcello Canali, Guiseppe Varni, Roberto Bruni, Virgilio Gottard.* Advance reports have said that this is the greatest operatic film to date. Dir.: Carmone Gallone. (Excelsia Films.) First shown at Rialto in late 1948.

Road to Heaven. Very simple, sincere Swedish " Miracle " film which is so unusual, so artless and so full of qualities not usually met with in the cinema that it is quite beyond criticism. Co-author is *Rune Lindstrom,* who plays the chief role in the picture. Dir.: Alf Sjoberg. First shown at the Academy in August 1948.

Shoe Shine. Another of the first-class post-war Italian movies. Based on a problem common enough in Italy, also to be found in any country suffering the aftermath of war. A tale of juvenile delinquency. About two boys (inseparable friends) who are caught dabbling in the black market, are sent to reform school. About their separation there, their gradual degradation and final tragedy. A shocking, moving, intensely realistic picture with the gloomy background of the dark, harsh life lived by the youngsters in their out-dated, grim prison. Cast : *Rinaldo Smordoni, Franco Interlenghi* (the two boys), *Aniello Mele, Bruno Ortensi, Pacifico Astrologo, Francesco de . Nicola, Antonio Carlino, Enrico de Silva, Antonio Lo Nigro, Angelo D'Amico, Emilio Cigoli, Giuseppe Spadaro, Leo Caravaglia, Luigi Saltamerenda, Maria Campi, Irene Smordoni, Anna Pedoni.* Dir.: Vittorio De Sica. Pro.: Paolo W. Tamburella. First shown at Rialto in Dec. 1947.

Spanish Serenade. The first Argentine (Spanish-speaking) picture to be seen generally in Britain turns out to be a conventionally made, quite polished and technically excellent story of life of the Spanish composer Albeniz, who seems to have had quite an adventurous time. Well acted and with a nice musical background. Cast : *Pedro Lopez Lager* (Albeniz) *Sabina Olmos, Amadeo . Novoa, Guillermo Contreros, Marisa Rogules, Carmelita Vasquez.* Dir.: Luis Cesar Amadori. (Argentine Sono Film.) First shown at La Continental, London, in June 1948.

Fred (Gar Moore) dreamily talks to Francesca (Maria Michi) of herself, as he knew her and makes her want to become again. From Episode 3, Rome, of the Robert (Open City) Rossellini directed PAISA.

Le Silence Est D'Or. Brilliant, witty, quite outstanding little French comedy written, produced and directed by Rene Clair; about two men friends and the one girl they both fall in love with, played against a background of the early days of movie-making. As one of the friends *Maurice Chevalier* makes a return to the screen after several years and gives a delightful, polished performance. Rest of cast : *Francois Perier, Marcelle Derrien, Dany Robin, Robert Pizani, Raymond Cordy, Paul Olivier, Roland Armontel.* Dir. and Pro.: Rene Clair. (R.K.O. Radio.) First shown at the Rialto in August 1948.

Un Revenant. The story of a famous choreographer (*Louis Jouvet*) who goes back to the town of his birth and at once gets caught up in the echoes of an old romance. Deciding to take revenge on those who plotted against him in the past, he is jerked back to sanity by a near-tragedy. Once again on the move, he tells his latest young protege that all women are alike, romance, broken hearts and revenge is just a lot of hot air. Rest of cast : *Gaby Morlay, Francois Perier, Ludmilla Tcherina, Marguerite Moreno, Jean Brochard, Louis Seigner.* Dir.: Chritian-Jaque. Pro.: Edouard Carles. First shown at the Academy in August 1948.

Vivere in Pace—To Live in Peace. One of the several outstanding films to come out of post-war Italy. How war came to a tiny village in the Italian mountains ; a first-class comedy that is always on the edge of drama, and becomes sheer tragedy at the end. A warmly human, very friendly film ; with a lovely background of the sunlit village, farmhouse and fields. Brilliantly acted by a cast headed by *Aldo Fabrizi* (the Priest of *Open City*). Rest of cast : *Gar Moore, Mirella Monti, John Kitzmiller, Heinrich Bode, Ave Ninchi, Ernesto Almirante, Nando Bruno, Aldo Silvani, Gino Cavalieri, Piero Palermini, Franco Serpilli.* Dir.: Luiga Zampa. Pro.: Carlo Ponti. (A Lux Pao film). First shown at Curzon in Oct. 1947.

ANTOINE ET ANTOINETTE was another prize-winner, taking the Cannes Festival Grand Prize in 1947. A comedy, the background was Paris of the working classes ; the plot concerned a lost-and-found winning lottery ticket. Here are A and A—Roger Pigaut and Claire Maffei.

The YEAR in the CINEMA

1948

(CONTINUED FROM PAGE 16)

came *A Double Life*, the Universal-International picture which won for star Ronald Colman the 1947-48 Oscar for the best male acting performance of the year on the screen. It was not an outstanding film, but it was quite an outstanding performance, good enough to give the film considerable distinction.

Now the flow increased somewhat. There was an excellent new boxing film entitled *Body and Soul* with John Garfield as the lad who fights his way from the gutter to the world of championships—all familiar enough, heaven knows, but very well done and therefore interesting. This same story was, incidentally, later to be repeated, more or less, in Metro-Goldwyn-Mayer's *Killer McCoy* with Mickey Rooney.

Then came *Gentleman's Agreement*—and here we had a really fine film. Like *Crossfire* before it, *Gentleman's Agreement* had as its theme the apparently prevalent American anti-Semitism. But, unlike *Crossfire*, it pulled no punches. The whole story centred on the question of racial prejudice. Gregory Peck gave a most sincere performance as the journalist who pretends he is a Jew so that he can get the true angle on his subject. Equally sincere was John Garfield as his Jewish friend,

Dorothy McGuire as his girl friend, and, in fact, the whole of the cast. The great point about *Gentleman's Agreement* was that quite apart from its subject it was a brilliant piece of film craft.

Another of the American pictures of this time was the best comedy we have seen since the beginning of the year, *Sitting Pretty*, in which Clifton Webb gave a very brilliant comedy performance as the most unusual baby-minder ever before seen on—or off—the screen! Another amusing comedy was R.K.O. Radio's *The Bishop's Wife*, which Londoners had a single previous opportunity of seeing last November (1947), when it was chosen for the Royal Command Film Performance and for which show the question of the tax was waived. In this movie Bishop David Niven prays for help and gets it—in the person of angel Cary Grant!

A less amusing, but tremendously effective, picture was *The Naked City*, the last production to be made by famous New York journalist Mark Hellinger before he died as the result of a heart attack. For this picture Hellinger, disdaining the studio, took his actors and cameras out into the city he loved so well and shot the entire film against the background of the actual New York streets and buildings. *Naked City* was a Whodunnit, but a Whodunnit with a very great difference. It never strained credulity and throughout the development of the man-hunt was completely logical. Barry Fitzgerald played the police inspector who tracks down the murderer of a dizzy blonde. Around this time we also saw *Forever Amber* which, as we all rather expected, came as a promised " bang " and went like a damp squib.

Bob Hope shares the top of the bill and all the fun and danger with Jane Russell in Paramount's The Paleface—in which our hero, the toughest pioneer who ever toted a gun, goes West—literally. Hope plays a " painless " dentist, Miss Russell plays " Calamity Jane ".

While these new American films were coming over we saw the British studios replying with some of their finest pictures of the year. About *Hamlet* much has been said and written, but the fact remains that it was a remarkably fine production and I don't think anybody could do anything but agree that if Shakespeare is to be brought to the screen then it could never be done in a better way than Laurence Olivier did it in the film he conceived, adapted, directed and produced as well as starred in. It was a *tour de force* for him and a prestige picture for Mr. Rank, who had backed its production with half a million out of his pocket.

Yet in spite of all the big guns which were fired during the *Hamlet* presentation I still feel that *Oliver Twist*, which followed it into Town a few weeks later, was actually a greater movie and the most important film to come from a British studio during 1948. Cineguild, who last year made that other Dickens classic, *Great Expectations*, into one of the greatest movies of the year, in *Oliver Twist* exceeded even their own previous best. *Oliver Twist* is great screen-craft, an outstanding example of the true meaning of film art. It lasts two hours, and, contrary to most films at the end of that period, leaves you—like its hero—wanting more !

The peak of the year seemed soon past, however, and then we had a series of average productions. But amongst the dross was occasional gold.

Technically speaking, Michael Powell and Emeric Pressburger's *The Red Shoes* was one of the most brilliant pictures of the year, its Technicolored ballet sequence being quite outstanding. *The World and His Wife* (*State of the Union* in America) was the new Capra ; rich, noisy talkie but most typical and entertaining. *The Pirate*, with Gene Kelly and Judy Garland, was the first Technicolored grand-scale musical we had since 1947.

Baines (that's Sir Ralph Richardson), butler at a foreign embassy in London, gives a sleeping tablet to Felipe (Bobby Henrey), the ambassador's small son, after he has been caught running away. A scene from the Carol Reed directed, London Films production called The Fallen Idol *(known formerly as* The Lost Illusion*).*

In October we had the first Carol Reed film since *Odd Man Out* (*Fallen Idol*, previously called *Lost Illusion*) and from Selznick came the first Technicolored Hitchcock film, *The Paradine Case*, with a cast including British Charles Laughton, Ann Todd, American Ethel Barrymore, Gregory Peck and lovely Italian newcomer Valli.

And here space demands that I bring these notes to a somewhat abrupt end. Forgive me if I have not mentioned *your* favourite film of the year ; in any case you'll find my comment about that in another section. In the nature of things these

Catherine Winslow (Margaret Leighton) asks Sir Robert Marton, K.C. (Robert Donat) a leading question in the London Films Production of the Terence Rattigan play The Winslow Boy. *Inset :* The Winslow *family takes the air (Margaret Leighton, Marie Lohr, Cedric Hardwicke, Neil North and Jack Watling).*

notes must be brief and sketchy but I hope I have in them at least given you something of an overall picture of some of the more interesting films and filmic events of 1948.

Since writing on page 9 about the deaths of two famous figures of the earlier cinema, Louis Lumière and Sergei Eisenstein, there has come the news of the death, in America, of David Wark Griffith. One of the great figures of the early motion picture, he came into it when the film was still little more than a flickering novelty and raised it by imagination and improvisation to the status of a young art. Griffith will for ever be remembered for his great epics of the silent screen, *Birth of a Nation, Intolerance, Broken Blossoms* and many others. It was Griffith who joined with Mary Pickford, Douglas Fairbanks and Charles Chaplin to form United Artists. His last movies, talkies, were not too successful and he appears to have spent his last years in plans which never reached fruition and the writing of his memoirs, in which he re-lived a great past. The modern cinema owes a very great deal to David Wark Griffith.

Douglas Fairbanks, Jr., tells Katie (played by Paule Croset) to flee while he stays to fight . . . . a scene from Universal-International's The Exile.

Rita Hayworth and Glenn Ford in The Loves of Carmen, *a Columbia picture.*

Frank Sinatra had the unusual role of a Catholic priest in the Miracle of the Bells, *an R.K.O. Radio picture. He is seen here with Fred MacMurray.*

First British feature film to be woven around the *Speedway* and the men who ride the cinders is the Wessex movie Once a Jolly Swagman in which Dirk Bogarde (centre) and Bonar Colleano (left) play riders and Sidney James (right) their team manager.

There's no real relationship between Bette Davis and new co-star Jim Davis, who share this scene from Warner's very talky Winter Meeting, Miss Davis's first film in two years.

Technically speaking, the Michael Powell and Emeric Pressburger production of The Red Shoes was the most interesting British picture of the year. Superbly made in Technicolor, its highspot was a full-length ballet, exquisitely danced by Moira Shearer (extreme right, seen here with Leonide Massine, centre, and Anton Walbrook) and photographed with artistic wizardry.

Edward Dryhurst's production of the Richard Llewellyn play Noose was the last film to star Carole Landis (seen here trying out a pair of knuckle dusters on gagged Joseph Calleia). Soon afterwards she went back to Hollywood and ended her life by suicide.

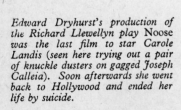

Countess Platen (Flora Robson) comes to tell Duke Ernest Augustus (Frederick Valk) that Konigsmark is in Sophie Dorothea's room, and asks for a warrant for his arrest. Inset : Stewart Granger as Konigsmark.

First large, spectacular Technicolored musical to reach the screen since the tax was imposed last year was Metro-Goldwyn-Mayer's The Pirate, in which Gene Kelly did some incredible dancing as well as singing with co-star Judy Garland.

Jack Read (Richard Attenborough) takes an interest in the shapely limbs of Lorna Beckett (Brenda Hogan) in the school bookshop. A scene from The Guinea Pig, a Boulting Brothers production for Pilgrim Pictures.

In Paramount's Dream Girl Betty Hutton (with Lowell Gilmore here) has a rare old time dreaming she's all kinds of girls in all kinds of lives—we see each of them in turn on the screen.

A PREVIEW OF THE 1949 RELEASES

I SUPPOSE there are many who would approach, compile and present such a feature as this without inward qualm or outward apology. Indeed, it is done ! Unfortunately, perhaps, I am not made of such stern stuff. I still feel as I have felt at this point of FILM REVIEW each year ; still consider that some word or two of explanation should be offered.

As I write 1948 is still in its middle age ; months will pass before any but the earliest releases of 1949 are actually fixed. But I cannot wait. *You* will expect your copy of FILM REVIEW to be in your hands, as usual, well before Christmas. Accordingly the publishers expect even this last section of the book to be in *their* hands by the very early autumn. So we must be British—and compromise.

In these pages I have illustrated some of those films which are pretty certain to be released some time during 1949 ; in fact, my main worry is that they may be brought forward into the 1948 release schedule. It may happen in isolated cases, as it has happened each year in the past. But at least I have spared no pains ; this time I have checked up direct with the American companies as well as with their offices over here. So if amongst these films you discover a 1948 release you will, I hope, realise that as this book was being written it was scheduled for showing *next* year and the cause of the apparent error is a change of plan made after FILM REVIEW had gone to press. Similarly if it happens the other way, if a film now booked for 1948 release and listed as such, is put back into the 1949 schedule.

(*Above*) What is likely to be one of the most interesting of the earlier 1949 releases is *R.K.O. Radio's* screen adaptation of the famous Eugene O'Neill play MOURNING BE-COMES ELECTRA. A drama of love and frustration, it is a decidedly " difficult " film subject. In bed is RAYMOND MASSEY, standing is ROSALIND RUSSELL and on the floor is KATINA PAXINOU.

(*Below*) LAUREN BACALL looks up, obviously a little worried about things, in *Warner's* KEY LARGO, a movie adapted from the 1939 Maxwell Anderson play concerning tough, ex-soldier HUMPHREY BOGART's cleaning up of a gang of crooks which includes EDWARD G. ROBINSON and LIONEL BARRYMORE.

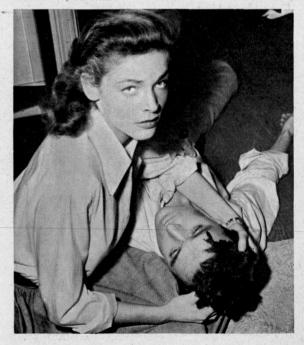

Inspector SYDNEY GREENSTREET questions star ROSALIND RUSSELL and other members of the cast of the play after their producer has been found murdered; from *R.K.O. Radio's* THE VELVET TOUCH, a farce-comedy. For the record, the lady on Miss Russell's right is ESTHER HOWARD. Standing next to FRANK McHUGH behind her is DAN FOSTER.

In any case, looking forward, at least with regard to the American movies, is more difficult than ever on this occasion. The new British quota act means that fewer films than ever before (apart from the 'blockade' during 1947-8) will come across the Atlantic next year. For those that do come over it will be quite a struggle to get a large, circuit booking. So, at the moment, the American companies are unwilling to commit themselves about the future. They know the films that are ready, are in production or are planned, but they cannot at the moment do more than hazard a fairly wide guess as to when, and even if, they will reach here.

But, with luck (I am crossing my fingers) as I have already said, I think you'll find all the American films illustrated in this section will be shown sometime during 1949.

As regards the British films, the 1949 position here is a little easier. Mr. Rank, with the comfortable knowledge that he has large numbers of cinemas in which to show his own films, and made even more sure of himself by the fact that the new quota will mean a better showing of his product in other, independent cinemas, has already laid his 1949 plan and as from him will come the great bulk of the year's productions I have asked **John C. Dennett,** his publicity director, to tell you something of the position. He writes:

"For 1949 the J. Arthur Rank Organisation has planned to provide cinema audiences throughout the world with 'a programme as fine as that of any

A rather suitable scene from *20th Century-Fox's* film SUMMER LIGHTNING with LON McCALLISTER romping with JUNE HAVER. The story is all about a boy who becomes owner of a champion mule team.

An unconventional family portrait; JEAN SIMMONS nurses the baby which has come so unexpectedly " out of the blue " while father (new star DONALD HOUSTON) watches with interest. From the *Launder and Gilliat* picture THE BLUE LAGOON.

One of the more spectacular scenes from the *Alexander Korda* production of BONNIE PRINCE CHARLIE; Highland Chieftains wait the arrival of the Clan Cameron, led by Jenny Cameron. (*Inset*) Flora Macdonald (MARGARET LEIGHTON) measures Prince Charles (DAVID NIVEN) for the dress in which he plans to escape.

other film organisation in any other part of the world. It represents an immense amount of work and real enthusiasm in the studios.' The quotation is from a statement made by Mr. J. Arthur Rank on June 9th, 1948.

" ' An immense amount of work '—this means no fewer than 60 feature productions to be shown this coming year, all except a few being made in the four studios well known to you—Denham, Pinewood, Gainsborough, and the associated Ealing Studios.

" From the conception of a film subject to its premiere may take from 6 to 9 months. 60 different first quality productions for one year, each needing at least 6 months work by large groups of people, all members of one Organisation. It is not an understatement, therefore, to say ' an immense amount of work.'

" If your memory is as long as the next man's, you will be able to recall the time when cinemagoers would not have wanted to cross the street to see a

It's a great—if somewhat expensive—compliment to a lady to fill her slipper with champagne and drink it. But it is just that compliment which VINCENT PRICE is paying DEANNA DURBIN in the Stetson House party scene of *Universal-International's* UP IN CENTRAL PARK.

Ealing's ANOTHER SHORE is another Irish film, based on a novel of the same title. Drinkers in this scene are STANLEY HOLLOWAY and ROBERT BEATTY.

Stop Press: Latest news to hand is that this film will be shown and probably generally released before the end of 1948.

British film. Now our films vie with the best in the world. The British film was rediscovered when it was able to express itself in terms of the British human saga.

"From these great pioneering days then to today. What are you likely to see *next* year?

"From Denham Studios, Two Cities Films, perhaps the greatest film of all time in Laurence Olivier's *Hamlet*, and among the fourteen others, Sid Field and Margaret Lockwood in a typical Sid Field comedy; John Mills in H. G. Wells's *The History of Mr. Polly*; Jean Kent in a Technicolor film of the gay nineties *Trottie True*; Stewart Granger in his first comedy—*Woman Hater*.

"From Pinewood, Independent Producers Ltd., among ten films, Jean Simmons in the Technicolor *The Blue Lagoon*; Ann Todd, Trevor Howard and Claude Rains in *The Passionate Friends*; a thriller as yet not finally cast—*The Trial of Madeleine*

Smith; and Dirk Bogarde whom you began to know in *Esther Waters* following in *Once a Jolly Swagman*.

"From among Sydney Box's twenty-one Gainsborough productions, I advise you to note Dennis Price in *The Bad Lord Byron*; *Cockpit* with Mai Zetterling, Richard Attenborough, William Hartnell, Mila Parely, Herbert Lom and Maxwell Reed; Fredric March in *Christopher Columbus*; Jack Warner, Kathleen Harrison and Susan Shaw in a series of the Hugget Family pictures; Googie Withers in *Once Upon a Dream*; and two action pictures—*Mantilla* in Technicolor, with a Spanish background, and *Turning Wheels*, to be made in Africa.

"From among Ealing's eight, John Mills in the true-to-life *Scott of the Antarctic*—a truly British picture which we are proud to present; Chips Rafferty in an outdoor Australian saga, *Eureka*

It was at her own request that Britain's No. 1 star MARGARET LOCKWOOD played the comparatively minor comedy role in the new SID FIELD comedy CARDBOARD CAVALIER. Sid plays a Cromwellian barrow boy.

(*Above*) APRIL SHOWERS is another *Warner* musical, a vaudeville back-stage story of the 1912 era. Here in this scene are ANN SOTHERN, ROBERT ALDA and JACK CARSON.

CHARLES BOYER, as the refugee doctor in Paris during the war, watches INGRID BERGMAN gamble. A scene from the film based on the Erich Maria Remarque novel ARCH OF TRIUMPH—*Metro-Goldwyn-Mayer*.

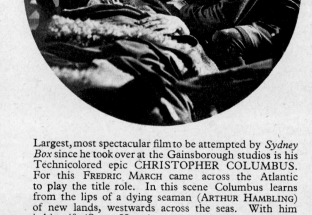

Stockade; a comedy with Basil Radford and Naunton Wayne; *Passport to Pimlico, Kind Hearts and Coronets* and *Whisky Galore.*

" Among our other activities there are three features which will gather strength in 1949—all of which are important to provide a complete cinema programme (the only film organisation in the world to do this).

" Gradually gaining first place in the world as the foremost unbiased documentary on home and overseas current affairs is the ' This Modern Age ' series. The object—to let you see and hear what is going on, in twenty minute stretches, about events of which you have read in the newspapers.

" You have seen and loved the wonderful cartoons which our American friends have produced to such

Largest, most spectacular film to be attempted by *Sydney Box* since he took over at the Gainsborough studios is his Technicolored epic CHRISTOPHER COLUMBUS. For this FREDRIC MARCH came across the Atlantic to play the title role. In this scene Columbus learns from the lips of a dying seaman (ARTHUR HAMBLING) of new lands, westwards across the seas. With him is his wife (SONIA HOLM).

When *Metro-Goldwyn-Mayer's* new film B.F.'s DAUGHTER arrives over here it will get a brand new title and you'll see it as POLLY FULTON ! *Metro-Goldwyn-Mayer* didn't know whether you might get the wrong idea of those initials, which haven't the same meaning in the U.S. In this scene of the dinner party you may be able to recognise BARBARA STANWYCK at the head of the table, CHARLES COBURN on her left, giving the toast, and SPRING BYINGTON sitting directly below him. Gentleman of this table, (you can see only the back of his head) is Miss Stanwyck's co-star VAN HEFLIN.

CLAUDE RAINS pours a drink for his wife, ANN TODD, while her lover, TREVOR HOWARD, watches her. It is at this moment in the film that the husband realises that he has been deceived. *Cineguild's* version of the H. G. Wells story THE PASSIONATE FRIENDS.

(*Above*) 20*th Century-Fox's* CAPTAIN FROM CASTILLE is an old-time Spanish adventure-romance (*circa* 1518) with hero TYRONE POWER saving heroine, new-star JEAN PETERS from a fate worse than death (!) Sharing this grassy bank, and scene, with them is LEE J. COBB.

good effect. This year will see the first of the British cartoons, which will be made by a group of hand-picked specialists operating in the company known as G.B. Animation.

"Thirdly, in our endeavour to use the cinema medium in the way considered to be the best for those of tender and susceptible imaginations, we shall produce more children's films, to be shown first in the Odeon and Gaumont-British cinema clubs in Britain, and subsequently in many other countries of the world.

"All this means many things, but most of all, perhaps, it means an industry, a British Film Industry employing thousands of people. For those at home there is a regular supply of good entertainment. For those abroad a sight of Britain and what Britain is doing that otherwise might not have reached them."

Going back for a final moment to the American films of 1949, I don't know what we *shall* be seeing but I do know what *I should like* to see. For instance, the long-promised Harold Lloyd-Preston Sturges comedy *The Sin of Harold Diddlebock* (originally promised for 1947 release !); *Bill and Coo*, the film with an all-bird cast which was such

a sensation in America, the musical *Easter Parade*, with Judy Garland as Fred Astaire's new partner, *Arch of Triumph*, with Bergman and Boyer co-starred, *The Snake Pit*, with Olivia de Havilland as an inmate of a mental asylum.

All these, and many more, which look so tremendously interesting on paper and which, we all hope, will prove as interesting on celluloid.

Metro-Goldwyn-Mayer's GOOD NEWS is a gay, Techni-colored collegiate musical comedy which re-introduces such old-time favourite numbers as "The Best Things in Life are Free." Here JUNE ALLYSON is somewhat obviously shocked at the wisp of a dress she is expected to wear.

Serenading with the guitar is ROBERT MITCHUM, while LORETTA YOUNG plays the piano and WILLIAM HOLDEN plays the role of a frowning spectator. A scene from *R.K.O. Radio's* RACHEL AND THE STRANGER.

"Quiet, please," orders JIMMY HANLEY, as he tries to write his article on goodwill for the local paper while his rowdy friends (GEOFFREY KEEN, LESLIE WESTON and CYRIL SMITH) go on repairing the bomb-blasted attic in which he lives; from the new Jeffrey Dell comedy for *Two Cities,* IT'S HARD TO BE GOOD.

They had their traffic problems in those days too . . . JOHN MILLS gets into trouble with his bicycle in this scene from his own production (for *Two Cities*) of the H. G. Wells story THE HISTORY OF MR. POLLY.

(*Above*) Glamorous red-headed ANN SHERIDAN co-stars for the first time with GARY COOPER in the Leo McCarey production for *R.K.O. Radio*, GOOD SAM. LOUISE BEAVERS is the coloured lady.

Though the revivals of two former DANNY KAYE films have been amongst the greatest fortune-making movies of the year, we have had no new Kaye film in 1948. But we are due to see his latest opus, the Preston Sturges directed SECRET LIFE OF WALTER MITTY, pretty early in 1949. With him in this *Samuel Goldwyn-R.K.O. Radio* production will be Danny's old co-star VIRGINIA MAYO.

Promised last year for this, but now put back until 1949 release is *Warner's* re-make of the idyllic tale ESCAPE ME NEVER, with IDA LUPINO playing the role taken in a previous film by Elisabeth Bergner. With her are co-stars ELEANOR PARKER and ERROL FLYNN.

1948 saw HERMIONE BADDELEY spring into sudden prominence on the screen, due to several outstanding character performances. Here she is in her biggest part to date, in the *Grand National* picture NO ROOM AT THE INN.

Stop Press : Latest news to hand is that this film will be shown and probably generally released before the end of 1948.

Anger flares up between FREDRIC MARCH and EDMOND O'BRIEN in this scene from the *Universal-International* film ANOTHER PART OF THE FOREST. Horrified onlooker is ANN BLYTH.

Originally scheduled for 1948 release, but later put back into the 1949 list, is *Warner's* VOICE OF THE TURTLE, a screen version of the John Van Druten play. Conversing are RONALD REAGAN and ELEANOR PARKER.

(Below) Starry trio in *Metro-Goldwyn-Mayer's* CASS TIMBERLANE are ZACHARY SCOTT, LANA TURNER and SPENCER TRACY.

SUMMER HOLIDAY is a musical re-make, in Technicolor, of the famous play and former film "Ah Wilderness." Sitting round *Metro-Goldwyn-Mayer's* table, left to right, are "BUTCH" JENKINS, SELENA ROYLE, MICKEY ROONEY, WALTER HUSTON, AGNES MOOREHEAD, FRANK MORGAN and SHIRLEY JOHNS.

Warners' ROMANCE ON THE HIGH SEAS is a Technicolored musical; in this scene you'll recognise DON DEFORE, JANIS PAIGE and S. Z. SAKALL.

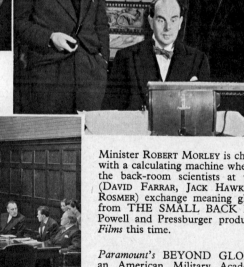

Minister ROBERT MORLEY is childishly impressed with a calculating machine when he comes to see the back-room scientists at work, while they (DAVID FARRAR, JACK HAWKINS and MILTON ROSMER) exchange meaning glances. A scene from THE SMALL BACK ROOM, the next Powell and Pressburger production, for *London Films* this time.

Paramount's BEYOND GLORY is a story of an American Military Academy, with cadet ALAN LADD (seated at table) falsely accused of cowardice. Standing, pointing to him, is GEORGE MACREADY, while seated opposite him is GEORGE COULOURIS.

(*Below*): *Metro-Goldwyn-Mayer's* THIS TIME FOR KEEPS brought together the late DAME MAY WHITTY (seated) with ESTHER WILLIAMS and JOHNNIE JOHNSTON.

Said to be an outstanding film for 1949 showing is *Warners'* THE TREASURE OF SIERRA MADRE, the quest for gold of three men and how its finding separately affects them. Here are HUMPHREY BOGART and WALTER HUSTON, whose son John Huston directed the film as well as wrote the screenplay.

DAN DAILEY and CHARLES WINNINGER (who gives one of the best performances of his career in the film) in *Fox's* GIVE MY REGARDS TO BROADWAY, a nostalgic, Technicolored story of a vaudeville family, enlivened with some suitable musical numbers.

HENRY FONDA and JAMES STEWART in A MIRACLE CAN HAPPEN, a starry *United Artists* portmanteau picture.

CHARLES COBURN wags an admonitory finger at PEGGY CUMMINS in a scene from the *20th Century-Fox* film GREEN GRASS OF WYOMING, which is another chapter in the life of " Thunderhead, Son of Flicka," the wild albino stallion created by Mary O'Hara in her famous series of books.

One of the films for which the more discerning moviegoer should watch for with particular interest is *R.K.O. Radio's* THE PEARL, adapted from a John Steinbeck story about a Mexican fisherman who finds a pearl and instead of peace and happiness finds with it only pain and delusion. In it PEDRO ARMANDARIZ is said to give his finest performance yet ; with him here is MARIA ELENA MARQUES.

SALLY GRAY, DEREK FARR and NIGEL PATRICK in *N. A. Bronsten's* production of SILENT DUST (tentative title still used at presstime), from a play about a father who thinks he has a hero son but finds instead he has a coward and a criminal.

(*Left*) ROBERT CUMMINGS feeds CLAUDETTE COLBERT with the assistance of chop-sticks—from SLEEP MY LOVE, a *United Artists* film.

On a previous page you read Walt Disney himself explaining his new feature-cartoon MELODY TIME. Here are four scenes from the picture : (a) shows the heroism of "Little Toot" the heroic tug of New York Harbour, (b) shows Cowboy Pecos Bill as a boy, a very tough young man, in (c) "Bumble Boogie" gets a shock when the flowers turn nasty on him, and (d) shows "Johnny Appleseed," planting one of the apple orchards he spaced along 10,000 miles of pioneer trails.

At the time of writing, MELODY TIME is due for London showing late 1948 or early 1949 with general release pretty certain to be in the first few months of '49.

The Final Word ....

Now that you have reached this last page of FILM REVIEW I hope you have enjoyed it. If you have a grievance, a suggestion for improving next year's book, or just want to point out where you think I am wrong, write to me. With your help I hope to make next year's FILM REVIEW a better one than this.

And at this moment I would like to put on record my sincere thanks for the continued wholehearted co-operation that has been shown me by the publicity departments of the film companies. They have all taken great pains to see that I have had what I wanted and nothing I asked was ever too much trouble.

F. Maurice Speed

Printed in Great Britain by L. T. A. Robinson Ltd., London, S.W.9